101
GREAT
RESUMES

Revised Edition

By
RON FRY

Winning Resumes for
Any Situation
Any Job
Any Career

CAREER
PRESS

Franklin Lakes, NJ

101 GREAT RESUMES, REVISED EDITION
EDITED BY NICOLE DEFELICE
TYPESET BY EILEEN DOW MUNSON
Cover design by Mada Design, Inc./NYC
Printed in the U.S.A. by Book-mart Press

To order this title, please call toll-free 1-800-CAREER-1 (NJ and Canada: 201-848-0310) to order using VISA or MasterCard, or for further information on books from Career Press.

The Career Press, Inc., 3 Tice Road, PO Box 687,
Franklin Lakes, NJ 07417
www.careerpress.com

Library of Congress Cataloging-in-Publication Data

Fry, Ronald W.
    101 great resumes : winning resumes for any situation, any job, any
career / by Ron Fry.— Rev. ed.
        p. cm.
    Rev. ed. of: 101 great resumes / Career Press editors. c1996.
    ISBN 1-56414-628-6 (paper)
    1. Résumés (Employment) I. Title: One hundred one great resumes.
II. Title: One hundred and one great resumes. III. Title.

HF5383 .A17 2002
650.14'2—dc21

                                                2002031565

TABLE OF CONTENTS

THE ELEMENTS OF YOUR RESUME

Resumes are dead, some will tell you. Don't need one, shouldn't make one, never send one.

Or you *still* need one, but not the one you're used to. Has to be scannable. E-mailable. Online. Even better, a multi-media presentation on your own Website!

Well…no. Resumes are *not* dead. The process *has* changed in some very key ways—slapping together a quick list of your jobs and schools and, oh, yeah, some of that volunteer stuff and extracurricular clubs, is not going to fly anymore (presuming it ever did). Speaking of "key," who ever heard of "key words" a decade ago? But then, we weren't posting our resumes on Hotjobs.com, either.

There are more and more qualified people out there for most jobs than in recent memory. So what's really changed is the level of competition and the need, more than ever, to set yourself apart from all those other contenders.

Nope, still need a resume. Just one that's going to require more preparation, better writing, and a more professional, eye-catching presentation.

Exactly what is a resume?

Your resume is a written (or e-mailed, scannable, or electronic) document that is intended to convince an employer that his needs and your skills and qualifications are a perfect match. Which doesn't mean you will immediately be offered the job, just that you will get in the door for an interview.

Your resume should describe you and show what you *can* do by highlighting what you have *already* done. It should include your professional and volunteer experience, special skills, education, and accomplishments.

What *shouldn't* your resume be? Informal, lengthy, unfocused, lacking in pertinent detail, glib, highly personal, chatty, dishonest, or overblown. Oh, and it shouldn't be a mix of 14 different type styles (with liberal use of boldface, italics, and underlines) printed on canary yellow or purple neon paper.

Who needs a resume? You do. Whatever your age, sex, marital status, religious persuasion, or hair color. Whether you're graduating from high school, college, or grad school; moving in, up, or out of a career; "transitioning" from one career to another (or from the military to anything); or reentering the workforce after any substantial interruption.

Did I omit your situation? Sorry—but you need a resume, too.

Even if you're a student just applying for a summer job, internship, or part-time work, a well-prepared, well-written, well-designed resume will set you apart, show prospective employers you're serious, and present you in the manner you want to be perceived—professional, competent, and ready to work.

What will it do for me?

An excellent resume will not get you a job all on its own. But it does demonstrate that you take yourself and your career seriously—that you've put the necessary time and thought into communicating your qualifications, accomplishments, and goals.

A good resume helps you pique a prospective employer's interest and prevents you from achieving circular-file status. Whether you're making a "cold" call or have already developed a contact within the company, your resume is the personal calling card that will help you market your skills and experience...and perhaps land you an interview.

In today's job market, networking is essential. Your friends, neighbors, relatives, and former co-workers are all significant contacts in the business world. Having a current resume comes in handy when Uncle James or Neighbor Nancy hears about a position right up your alley. Circulating your resume among your network increases your chances of landing gainful employment.

Your resume also serves as a self-assessment tool, an opportunity to complete a self-inventory and see where you've been and where you'd like to go. Creating your resume allows you to evaluate your career and set future goals.

What is an effective resume?

An effective resume must make a good first impression. Of course, appearance is important. Typos, grammatical mistakes, and dog-eared pages will not impress many prospective employers.

But content is even more crucial. The information in your resume needs to be well organized, easy to read, and results-oriented.

An effective resume should:

▶ **Address the employers' needs.** Employers hire people who can fill *their* specific needs. Communicate that *you* are that person. At this point, you shouldn't even be thinking about *your* needs, wants, or desires…I guarantee you the employer isn't!

▶ **Show employers how they will benefit**. Stress your accomplishments and show employers you're an excellent prospect with talents to spare. Provide results-oriented data that proves you've handled previous jobs well and have consistently contributed to the success of every company, group, or club with which you've associated.

▶ **Be clear and concise.** Employers sort through piles of resumes daily and typically devote 30 seconds *or less* to each one. Make your presentation clear, concise, and easy to read.

▶ **Be targeted.** Your resume should communicate a well-defined objective tied to a specific career (even if you don't actually include a "Job Objective").

▶ **Support your promises of performance with reasons why you are the best applicant.** Clearly present your skills and qualifications.

▶ **Be realistic.** It should describe a person qualified and suited for the particular career it has targeted. Shy introverts should not try to present themselves as killer salespeople; anal-retentive accountants should not be seeking creative jobs at the trendiest ad boutique.

▶ **Be honest.** Many of you may be tempted to make that one short-term job—from which you were fired—effectively "disappear" from your resume by "adjusting" time spent at a previous and/or subsequent job. Or you will shamelessly inflate a low-level position into a fancier sounding title with greater responsibilities. The truth will out. Be careful.

▶ **Organize your job search**. A good resume helps you focus on your accomplishments and career goals. It also helps organize your thoughts for potential job interviews. Once you've taken stock of yourself, and realized all you've achieved and what you have to contribute, you will enter the job interview and networking process with much more confidence.

When should I start preparing?

Many professionals who have prepared a variety of different resumes during their careers make it a habit to keep at least a generic resume up-to-date, so that it always reflects their current job title and responsibilities, educational level, job-related skills, key awards and honors, publications, memberships, and activities. At the very least, they make sure pertinent data is kept in appropriate files for inclusion on any updated resume. Whenever they need a "new" resume, it's a relatively simple matter of updating an already existing format.

Students and those of you leaving the military or reentering the workforce after a substantial interruption need far more time to prepare, write, format, and proof (and proof and proof) the series of targeted resumes you will need.

Series? You mean, more than *uno*? Yes, sorry, but every specific position for which you're applying requires a different resume. Maybe not *radically* different—a professional-looking format can often be utilized for a wide variety of job descriptions. But what you include and omit, what you emphasize and ignore, even some of the words you use will indeed be different.

So give yourself the time to really think about what you're doing and make sure the result—a professional resume perfectly targeted to the job you seek—has been worth your expected effort. Allow a month to collect and summarize all the data you need, then another month to prepare whatever number of resumes you need. Needless to say, as your job search progresses, you may find yourself creating new resumes for new opportunities. These, of course, will not take much time at all.

What if you aren't 100 percent sold on any single profession or even a particular industry? Can't really say what the heck you want to be when you grow up? Or are contemplating a career change but are unsure of its exact direction or parameters?

Take the time to *think* before you plunge into the job-search process, let alone the resume-preparation process, to crystallize your objectives and solidify your goals. Tackle the nuts and bolts of preparing your resume(s) only *after* you've made the key decisions about the direction of your career.

The information you need

At this stage, don't worry about having your records perfectly arranged and categorized. Don't even worry about having your entries in the right order. There are no extra points awarded for organization right now. Your immediate goal should be to get your accomplishments and experience on a few pieces of paper—the forms I've included on pages 17 to 24. In the next chapter, you'll learn how to manage this trove of information and how to highlight the qualifications and accomplishments that will be most meaningful to each prospective employer.

But there is a lot of information to organize, so the first step is to designate a single location in which to store all your records. Losing important transcripts, citations, or letters will simply lengthen the process and, in some cases, inhibit your ability to construct a perfect resume. I suggest creating a separate file folder for each major segment of information (with the appropriate filled-out summary form included, of course) using the following categories:

I. Work and volunteer experience

Review all of your work experience, whether it's babysitting for the neighbors or overseeing a multi-million dollar marketing budget for a Fortune 100 company. Remember, every job counts, whether it was part-time or full-time, paid, or unpaid.

You will need the following information for each job. (Although it eventually may be recorded, utilized, and/or presented differently, you'll need the *same* information for any volunteer activities—again, paid or unpaid.)

- ❏ Name, address, telephone number, fax number, and e-mail address of company.
- ❏ Name, title, and e-mail address of your direct supervisor.
- ❏ Exact dates worked (or involved).
- ❏ Approximate number of hours per week.
- ❏ *Specific* duties and responsibilities.
- ❏ *Specific* skills utilized.
- ❏ *Specific* accomplishments.
- ❏ Honors.
- ❏ Copies of awards.
- ❏ Letter(s) of recommendation.

Responsibilities

Write a brief description of your responsibilities at each job, but don't go into too much detail—just summarize what you did in each position. For example, if you're a salesperson looking to move into sales management with a new company, your prospective employer will be interested in knowing:

- ▶ How many people you supervised.
- ▶ If you managed a budget and, if so, its size.
- ▶ The amount of revenue for which you were directly (and indirectly) responsible.
- ▶ The size of your sales territory.

This information will give employers a clear idea of the kind and scope of responsibilities you can handle. Consequently, it's especially important to consider those responsibilities that are most applicable to your chosen field or targeted position.

Accomplishments

After summarizing your responsibilities, list your accomplishments *in specific terms*.

What did you do on that job, project, or team, and what were the specific results? Did you increase profits? Cut expenses? Beat projections? Stay on or under budget?

Did you solve a problem? Exceed a goal? Improve product performance? Improve productivity or efficiency?

Here's an example: In just two years, Anne revolutionized the production function at her company's manufacturing plant. Even while understaffed, she managed to exceed production schedules and objectives and turn out a nearly defect-free product. These are major accomplishments that deserved to be a prominent part of her resume. Here's how she concisely expressed them:

- *Exceeded production schedules while manufacturing a 99.5% defect-free product.*
- *Surpassed objectives by 25% while 15% understaffed.*

If you're having trouble identifying specific individual accomplishments, consider departmental- or even company-wide projects in which you participated. Did your group supply the financial statistics that helped determine whether a key project should proceed? Did you serve on the team that evaluated your company's current computer system? Perhaps you found upgrading the systems would provide needed services and the company wouldn't have to buy a whole new system. That's something to brag about, in specific terms.

Also consider any work-related award that might reflect your accomplishments. Did you win an achievement award for writing the "New Employee Orientation Handbook"? Why? Was it because supervisors found that new employees who read the book had a better understanding of where they fit in and how they could contribute to the company's goals and targets? That's an accomplishment! Don't leave it out!

A final, brief note on listing both responsibilities and accomplishments: As you begin to jot things down, don't begin your entries with "Responsible for." Instead, use "action" words, such as *designed, created, directed, handled, achieved, supervised, coordinated,* or *implemented* for greater impact. (See p. 40 for a great list of power words.)

Volunteer experience

Just because you weren't paid to do something doesn't mean you didn't gain valuable experience that should be included on your resume. You may be so used to equating "work" with "pay" that you are discounting key accomplishments merely because they were part of your volunteer activities. Did you manage the budget and purchasing for an organization's fund-raising supper, recruit volunteers for the library book sale, or organize a musical program for the senior center? Organize a charitable car wash, direct other volunteers in a clean-up effort or paint posters and signs? Just because you didn't receive a paycheck for performing these functions doesn't mean they don't count!

The less actual work experience you have, the more "work" your volunteer experience has to do on your resume. If you have little or no paid work experience, or if you've been out of the job market and are preparing to reenter, you have no choice but to "translate" your volunteer activities into "work experience." List responsibilities, accomplishments, honors, and awards just as if they were "real" jobs. And quantify results wherever possible. Don't create entries that are misleading or untrue, but be sure to take credit for what you actually did.

For example, did your campaign drive for the women's symphony unit increase membership? How much? Did you serve on the committee that designed a community program for developing good parenting skills?

Here's how you would feature these achievements:

- *Recommended and organized membership drive for new women's symphony unit; increased membership 35%.*

- *Designed, coordinated and presented "Developing Good Parenting Skills" program to fill a community need. Program has evolved into 150 volunteers and nearly 500 participants and earned state and county Division of Child and Family Services (Welfare) awards.*

Don't discount *any* contribution you may have made, even if you weren't in a leadership role. Employers want to hire productive people. Your volunteer service will show that you're an active person and enhance the chances of your resume landing in the "possible candidate" pile rather than the circular file.

2. Education

For all but recent graduates, the educational listing will usually be fairly brief. You'll want to include the name and location of each school you attended, date of graduation, and your degree or major area of study. If you didn't graduate, note the years you attended the school and the type of courses you completed. For example:

- *Purdue University, West Lafayette, IN*
  20 credit hours in Aeronautical Engineering (1998-2000)
- *Courses in Elementary Education*
  University of Michigan, Ann Arbor, 2000-2002

If you're a recent high school, trade school or college graduate, you may want to list a few of the courses you completed, especially if you have little or no work or volunteer experience. But don't go too far afield. Just list those that apply to the position or field you're considering.

You may also need to play up your school activities and extracurricular accomplishments. Were you president of the chess club or drum major for the band? Maybe you performed an audit to fulfill a class requirement. Whatever the case, include such information on your resume, and *be specific* about your accomplishments. For example:

- *Led high school marching band to regional championship; won award for outstanding direction as drum major.*
- *Recommended new schedule for Big Ten chess tournament, which reduced travel time and lost school hours.*
- *Performed audit of company with 500 employees to fulfill class requirement; recommended new computerized bookkeeping software, which reduced data-entry time and provided more detailed reports.*

You may also want to draw attention to unusual challenges you met, such as earning stellar grades while working nearly full-time to earn all of your college expenses.

Your GPA and class rank

If you've been employed for several years, your high school and college grades are virtually insignificant to a prospective employer. After 10 or 20 years in the work force, your experience and accomplishments should speak for themselves. Except for possibly ensuring you meet the minimal educational requirements for the position, most recruiters will barely glance at anything else you include under "Education."

However, if you're recently out of school and your grades are good, feel free to include them in the educational section. Be sure to include the scale on which your grade point average (GPA) was determined. For example, include your GPA if it was 3.0 or higher on a 4.0 scale (3.0/4.0) and 4.5 or higher on a 6.0 scale (4.5/6.0). If the GPA in your major area of study was substantially better than your overall GPA, you may consider highlighting it instead, especially if your major is directly related to the job you're seeking.

If you graduated with honors, mention it in your degree listing, but then omit your GPA. If your class rank is more impressive than your GPA, you may use it instead.

Here are a few examples:

- *B.S., Computer Science, 2001, Tempe University, Tempe, AZ (3.8/4.0)*
- *Bachelor of Arts in Mass Communication,* with honors, *1999, Boston University*
- *Decatur High School, Decatur, FL, 2002. Ranked 4th in class of 300*

If you took some courses that aren't related to your degree but are specific to your new career goal, go ahead and profile them under your degree information.

For example, while finishing your degree in agricultural economics, you took several electives in political science. Your major aside, you're interested in pursuing a career as a legislative aide. Here's how to get the best of both worlds:

> *B.S. Agricultural Economics, Iowa State University, Ames (2002),*
> *18 credit hours in political science*

Internships, co-op work, and foreign exchange experience

If you are a recent graduate, cite any internships, whether for pay or class credit. You'll probably want to include your internship accomplishments under the Experience heading, but you can decide that later. For now, just gather the information. Here are some sample listings:

> *B.S., Accounting, 2001, University of Delaware, Newark*
> - *One-semester audit internship at DuPont corporate headquarters, Wilmington, DE*
> - *Three credit-hour internship in accounting for Registrar's Office, University of Delaware, Newark*

Many students are involved with co-op work experiences while in college. Again, your accomplishments may be best presented in the Experience section.

However, if you decide to list them under Education (perhaps you've been in the work force for several years), follow the above example and substitute your co-op information. Your co-op experience shows you'll take that extra step to achieve your career goals.

Experiences as a foreign exchange student are also worth noting. Although they may not be related to your career goal, the fact that you studied abroad shows you are unafraid to confront new challenges.

Here's a sample listing:

> *B.A., Personnel Management, DePauw University, Greencastle, IN (1999)*
> *One year foreign study at Athens University, Greece*

3. Licensing, certification, and special skills/training

It's important to list any licenses or certifications to show the employer you're trained for the job, especially if you're in a skilled trade, such as an airline mechanic or dental assistant, or a profession in which a license of certification is required, such as teaching.

While you'll be listing your qualifications and accomplishments under another heading, this section gives you the opportunity to indicate when you received your training and/or certification.

For professional licenses and certification, include:

❑ Name and type of license.

❑ State (or states) in which it is valid, if applicable.

❑ Date of certification.

❑ Number of the license, if appropriate.

Here are a few examples:

> *NALA Certified Legal Assistant, 1999*
> *Virginia Teaching Certification, secondary education, 1998*
> *Expanded Duties Dental Assistant Certification, 2001*
> *Nevada Real Estate License, 2002*

For special training, include the name of the course, where you took it, and the date you completed training. For example:

> *Radiograph Certification, Indiana University School of Dentistry,*
> *Bloomington, IN, 1999*
> *Certificate in Litigation and Trial Practice, The Paralegal Institute,*
> *Los Angeles, CA, 2001*

You also might want to mention any on-the-job or special job-related training you've received, such as completing a computer course. You could highlight it as follows:

> *CAD software: 2-month training program,*
> *NASA Computer Training Center, Hampton, VA, 1999*

However, there's no need to merely list attendance at professional or personal-development seminars, such as those that explain effective team-building techniques or how to enhance your self-esteem. No doubt you picked up valuable information from such courses, but just completing them isn't necessarily a particularly noteworthy accomplishment.

4. Military experience

If you served in the military, it should almost always be included on your resume (barring a dishonorable discharge or a prolonged stint in the stockade). Your special training and accomplishments are valuable, especially if they relate directly to your chosen civilian career. Many employers consider the discipline, character, leadership and team-building skills developed through military training to be a big plus, so the more you achieved (and the longer you served), the more detail you should include. This is especially true if your only experience is *in* the military.

Be sure to list the following information for each tour of duty:

❑ Branch and dates of service.

❑ Final rank achieved.

❑ Duties and responsibilities.

❑ Awards, citations and medals.

❑ Details of special training and/or schooling.

❑ Specific skills developed.

❑ Specific accomplishments.

5. Memberships and activities

Here is your opportunity to list any memberships and activities you haven't already covered under Work Experience. Your activities don't necessarily have to be career-related. If most of them are, you may want to consider using the heading "Professional Affiliations."

If you are an inveterate "joiner," don't feel it necessary to list *every* membership. Taking up valuable resume space to list organizations to which you just send an annual dues check is questionable. And if any are religious or political in nature, you may want to omit them entirely. Why invite prejudice when you don't have to?

Just focus on the ones you think would benefit an employer and those that are related to your career. As discussed earlier, employers are looking for "doers"—productive people. Your activities will show that you're a well-rounded person with interests outside of work.

On the other hand, if you have little or no actual work experience but a plethora of experience with your church, synagogue, temple, or a service group, you may consider giving them more attention. What choice do you have?

(On the *other* other hand, you may agree with some resume experts who counsel omitting all such extraneous information. Personally, I would omit all but the clear-cut, career-related activities.)

Whatever you decide to include or omit, any listing should be current and brief. Just include the names of the organizations and any leadership positions you currently hold.

Here are two examples:

> *Treasurer, Lion's Club*
> *President, Board of Directors, Akron Community Theater*

6. Awards and honors

For the most part, you've probably characterized any work-related awards or volunteer honors as accomplishments in the Work Experience or Volunteer Experience sections. However, if you've received any other award that you think the employer will view as a benefit, list it here. Just remember that many employers will take less than 30 seconds to review your resume—they may never even get to this section.

If the honor is really important, you probably should move it to either the Work Experience or Volunteer Experience section where it's more likely to get noticed. And if it's an academic honor, such as membership in Phi Beta Kappa, a prestigious scholarship or fellowship, even membership in the National Honor Society or making the Dean's list, give it the prominence it deserves in the Education section.

7. Specific skills and talents

You should include a section highlighting these if they are particularly notable and job-related, especially if they coincide with the qualifications posted for the job at hand. Whether you can type like a demon, design Websites in your sleep, speak a handful of languages, or are a scratch golfer, you should at least list every talent and skill on the forms on pages 23-24. For each, include:

❑ Description of skill.

❑ Specific training in it.

❑ Years of experience.

❑ Level of expertise.

❑ Accomplishments related to it.

Some skills may be unimportant for many jobs but essential for the one you are pursuing. Are you a certified scuba instructor? A potential employer in the banking industry may not care, but if you're interested in a tourism job in the Caribbean, that special skill could be a big point in your favor!

Two areas of expertise that virtually demand prominent placement: Computer skills and teaching or training experience. Obviously the former should be a key part of your resume if you are applying for any job that is highly technical. But computer skills are a plus no matter what career you're pursuing or what job you're interviewing for, even if they were not mentioned as a pertinent qualification.

Any teaching or training experience should be included, even if the "experience" was conducting a one-day workshop for your two-person department. The ability to present and communicate ideas is highly prized, and teaching experience of any kind will often be interpreted as a sign of leadership.

Were you the keynote presenter at an industry function. Are you often asked to speak at seminars or meetings? Have you authored a book? A journal article? An article for a major magazine?

While some professions would consider published articles an essential qualification for almost any job (college professors, for one), being able to tout a speech, article, book, or major presentation is clearly something a reasonable percentage of your competitors will be unable to match.

In summary

No doubt your experience and achievements seem more significant now that you've taken the time to gather them all together. This exercise is a great boost to the ego!

Before you move on, take the time to review each section and make sure you've included every bit of applicable information. When you get ready to draft your resume, you may choose not to include some data, but at least you'll have options. In the next chapter, you'll decide what to include and how best to present it.

1. Work Experience

(Make one copy of the worksheet for each paid job or professional
internship position you have held.)

1. Name of company _____

2. Address _____

_____

3. Phone and fax numbers _____

4. E-mail _____

5. Your job title (Use the actual title that would be on employee records.)

_____

6. Start and end dates (month and year) _____

7. Salary (beginning and end) _____

8. Supervisor's name and title _____

_____

9. Supervisor's e-mail _____

10. General job description (one- or two-sentence summary of your job)

_____

_____

_____

_____

_____

11. Responsibilities
    Management/supervisory duties (include size of staff and specific duties—hiring,
    training, etc.) _____

_____

_____

Budgetary/financial duties (include any duties related to money—writing a budget,
totaling daily receipts, analyzing cost/profit ratios, etc.) _____

_____

_____

_____

Sales/marketing duties (include specifics about product sold, type of customer base, advertising responsibilities, long-term marketing planning, etc.)

_____

_____

_____

_____

Customer service (include number of customers you served on a regular basis, plus their "status"—retail customer, executive-level clients, etc.)

_____

_____

_____

_____

Production duties (include amount of goods/services produced on a daily, monthly, or annual basis) _____

_____

_____

_____

Technical duties (include any duties that required you to use computers or other technical equipment) _____

_____

_____

_____

Other _____

_____

_____

12. Accomplishments (include honors and awards) _____

_____

_____

_____

13. Special skills learned (computer skills, telephone sales, desktop publishing, etc.)

_____

_____

_____

_____

2. Volunteer Experience

(Make one copy of this worksheet for each volunteer position you have held.)

1. Name of organization _____

2. Address _____

_____

3. Phone and fax numbers _____

4. E-mail _____

5. Position/title (if no position held, simply indicate "member")

_____

6. Start and end dates of this position _____

7. Start and end dates of your membership (month and year)

_____

8. Hours devoted per week _____

9. Name(s) of organization president(s) or your ranking superior

_____

10. President's or superior's e-mail _____

11. General job description (one- or two-sentence summary of your job)

_____

_____

_____

_____

12. Responsibilities
    Management/supervisory duties (include size of staff and specific duties—coordinating, training, etc.) _____

_____

_____

_____

Budgetary/financial duties (include any duties related to money—writing a budget, totaling sales receipts, analyzing cost/profit ratios, etc.) _____

_____

_____

_____

Sales/marketing duties (include specifics about product sold, type of customer base, advertising responsibilities, long-term marketing planning, etc.)

_____

_____

_____

_____

Customer service (include number of "customers" you contacted on a regular basis, plus their "status"—high school students, disabled adults, community leaders, etc.) _____

_____

_____

_____

Production duties (include amount of goods/services produced on a daily, monthly, or annual basis) _____

_____

_____

_____

Technical duties (include any duties that required you to use computers or other technical equipment) _____

_____

_____

_____

Other _____

_____

_____

13. Accomplishments (include honors and awards)

_____

_____

14. Special skills learned (computer skills, telephone sales, desktop publishing, etc.)

_____

_____

_____

3. Education

High school education

(If you have many years of experience under your belt, you need only complete questions 1-6 for high school education.)

1. School name _____

2. Address (city and state) _____

3. Years attended/year graduated _____

4. GPA/class rank _____

5. Honors (valedictorian, Top 10%, scholarship recipient, etc.)

    _____

6. Accomplishments _____

    _____

7. Major courses _____

8. Special skills learned _____

    _____

Post-secondary education

(List here college, trade school, and postgraduate work.)

1. School name _____

2. Address (city and state) _____

3. Years attended _____

4. Year graduated and degree earned _____

5. GPA/class rank _____

6. Honors (valedictorian, Top 10%, scholarship recipient, etc.)

    _____

7. Accomplishments _____

    _____

8. Major courses _____

9. Special skills learned _____

    _____

4. Other Training

(List any additional vocational courses, on-job training, licenses, or certifications.)

1. Training received/license or certification earned _____

_____

2. Name of training institution _____

3. Address and phone number _____

_____

4. Start and end dates of training _____

5. Name and title of instructor _____

6. Skills learned_____

_____

_____

_____

7. Accomplishments _____

_____

_____

1. Training received/license or certification earned _____

_____

2. Name of training institution _____

3. Address and phone number _____

_____

4. Start and end dates of training _____

5. Name and title of instructor _____

6. Skills learned_____

_____

_____

_____

7. Accomplishments _____

_____

5. Military Service

1. Branch _____

2. Rank _____

3. Dates of service _____

4. Duties _____

_____

_____

_____

_____

5. Special skills learned _____

_____

_____

_____

_____

6. Accomplishments (include awards, citations, medals)

_____

_____

_____

6. Special Skills

1. Name of skill _____

2. Specific training received _____

_____

_____

3. Years of experience _____

4. Level of expertise _____

5. Accomplishments related to this skill

_____

_____

_____

1. Name of skill _____

2. Specific training received _____

_____

_____

3. Years of experience _____

4. Level of expertise _____

5. Accomplishments related to this skill

_____

_____

_____

1. Name of skill _____

2. Specific training received _____

_____

_____

3. Years of experience _____

4. Level of expertise _____

5. Accomplishments related to this skill

_____

_____

1. Name of skill _____

2. Specific training received _____

_____

_____

3. Years of experience _____

4. Level of expertise _____

5. Accomplishments related to this skill

_____

_____

_____

Making Order Out of Chaos

Now that you've gathered, recorded, and filed the information for your resume, there's no doubt you're itching to get started on the first draft.

But before you do, you'll need to consider how to organize and present all that information to its greatest advantage. There are three basic formats from which to choose:

The chronological format

If you were to walk into any recruiter's office and rifle through the stack of resumes on her desk, you'd quickly notice that most of them utilized the chronological format. It's the "traditional" format and, for many of you, the "safe" choice, because it's the one with which many employers feel most comfortable.

A basic chronological format includes (in the following order):

1. Name header.

2. Objective (optional).

3. Summary of Qualifications or Profile (optional).

4. Work Experience/Employment

5. Education.

6. Other (Military Service, Awards, Professional Affiliations, Memberships, Activities, Publications, Skills, as appropriate).

It organizes your employment history by date, beginning with your most recent position and working backwards. For each position, you will provide the following information:

❑ Employer's name and location.

❑ Dates of employment.

❑ Your position/title.

❑ Your responsibilities and accomplishments.

In a chronological format, information about your work experience typically makes up about 70 percent of the resume. This section usually appears after the Job Objective or Skills Summary, if you've included either. However, if your educational background is the most important qualification for the position you're seeking, you may want to put the Education section first and then list your work experience.

You also can use this format to profile your volunteer experience. Just list volunteer positions the same way you would paid positions, including the name of the organization, the year(s) of involvement, your position, and your responsibilities and accomplishments.

The chronological format aims to clearly identify where you've been and what you've done that qualifies you for the job. It works best when:

▸ You have a stable history of paid employment or volunteer work.

▸ You've worked in the same general field for several years and are pursuing employment in that area.

▸ You have advanced steadily throughout your career and can show a consistent increase in level and responsibility.

▸ You have had few career changes and have spent a year or more at each of your jobs.

Here's how to create *your* perfect chronological resume, element by element:

Name header

The name header, which tells employers who you are and how to reach you, is always at the top of your resume. If you want to make it especially noticeable, set the header—or just your name—in bold face. There is no particular formatting "standard"—feel free to center, right- or left-justify this information.

Include your full name (first and last names and middle initial), your street address and phone number. Whatever phone number you include must be answered 24/7. Buy an answering machine or hire an answering service if necessary, but do *not* expect an employer to try to reach you more than once. The easier you make it for the employer to contact you, the better, so feel free to include your cell-phone number, pager, personal fax, e-mail address, and/or Website address.

I personally recommend including an e-mail address. More and more executives in the last few years have replaced phone calls with e-mail, since they can get a lot of information out (and leave a lot of messages) without dealing with busy signals and long answering-machine introductions. If it's *their* preferred mode of communication, make it yours. If you don't have an e-mail address, you can get one—free—from virtually any Internet Service Provider (ISP) or major site (AOL, Netscape, Yahoo, etc.).

If you feel comfortable receiving calls at work, list your work ⟩ (Keep in mind that many recruiters will frown on your use of work t͟ new job, unless your current employer is aware of your search. Th͟ you'll eventually treat them the same way, and they don't like it.) If not, ͟ home number and make sure an answering machine or voice-mail service is ͟ to capture any and every call. Prospective employers will usually call during bu͟ ness hours, the same time you'll be working. So make sure you don't miss thei͟ calls.

If you decide to use an answering machine, record a professional outgoing message and state your full name so employers know they've reached the right number. (Now is *not* the time to show off your incredible sense of humor with a phone message featuring your animal impressions.) Otherwise, they may not leave a message. Return any calls immediately.

If you are a college student with a temporary campus address (or, for that matter, anyone with a temporary address), list temporary and future addresses, phone numbers, and dates you can be reached at each address and/or number.

Objective (optional)

This is a brief statement that describes the kind of job you want, preferably in verbiage more exciting than a soup-can label.

You don't *have* to include a Job Objective. In fact, many resume writers would applaud if you didn't. A good resume should be attuned to what employers want, not what *you* want. And targeting a single objective may lead a screener to eliminate you from consideration for any other jobs at her firm, jobs you would *want* to be considered for…if you only knew they existed.

Yet there *are* circumstances where including a concise, highly targeted objective may make sense:

▶ **If you *are* only interested in one specific job.** If you're absolutely convinced there's only one job for you, then by all means state your precise objective and go for it.

▶ **If you're trying to send your career in a direction your experience doesn't seem to directly support.** If you are interested in altering your current career trajectory or in switching careers entirely, a well-written objective could clarify your plan and even offer support for it: "To help a public relations firm meet its clients' marketing communication needs by using the news sense and editing abilities developed during 15 years in magazine publishing."

If you decide to use an objective, put it right under the Name Header and title it Objective, Job Objective, or Career Objective.

State exactly the type of position you want, preferably in a dozen words or less. Show the employer you're focused on your career goal.

For example, the following objective is far too general and doesn't really communicate anything but *your* desires:

- *To apply my experience and knowledge, enhance my management skills, and develop professionally with a growth-oriented company.*

How would that set you apart from the hundreds of others seeking the same position? And what does it offer the employer? Compare its effect to these more targeted examples:

- *Computer programmer specializing in computer-aided automobile design*
- *Product account manager for a dental products distributor*

Summary of qualifications/skills (optional)

The Qualifications Summary, though optional, provides an excellent opportunity to draw attention to your most pertinent skills and experience in an attempt to convince an employer to read the rest of your resume. Every entry should be as targeted as your job goal and highlight specific experience, skills and training directly related to the position you're seeking.

Place your summary immediately after the Name Header or Objective (if you've used one) and call it Skills Summary, Summary of Qualifications, Experience Summary, or such. It can be in either paragraph or "bullet" form. If you decide to use a paragraph, restrict it to two or three short sentences:

Award-winning graphic artist–five years experience with state-of-the-art technologies on IBM and Macintosh systems. Skilled in video production and computer-generated images. Software knowledge includes Adobe Photoshop, Adobe Freehand, Adobe Premier, PageMaker, Adobe Illustrator, and Quark.

Strong background in metallurgy, including several internships with a leading engineering firm and two published articles in professional journals. Thorough knowledge of computer modeling techniques and programming.

If you decide on a "bulleted" format, list four or five points, such as:

- *10 years legal experience in product liability, medical malpractice, contracts, real estate, and personal injury litigation.*
- *Trained and experienced in photography, investigation, and interviewing techniques.*
- *Strong computer skills, including detailed knowledge of Microsoft Word, Access, Excel, and Quark Express.*
- *NALA certified.*

Sometimes it's more productive to complete the rest of your resume, determine your strong points, then go back and write your Summary of Qualifications. However you choose to handle such a summary, remember to always put your most important and relevant qualifications first.

Experience

The Experience section of your resume will most likely take up ⸃ chunk of space, because it is the section employers are most interested chronological format, this section may well represent 70 percent of the resume.

You have a couple of options here, depending on your situation. This section isn't necessarily just for paid work experience. It's a great place to include your volunteer work.

Here are three possible ways to organize your experience:

1. **List paid and volunteer positions separately.** For paid positions, use headings such as "Employment History" or "Professional Experience." Use "Volunteer Experience," "Related Experience," or "Other Experience" to highlight your volunteer positions. Place one section immediately after the other. (Whichever section includes the greatest support for your job goal should be given top billing.)

2. **Combine volunteer and paid positions.** Combining your volunteer and paid experiences can be quite effective, especially when both are targeted toward your job goal, or when the combination blends two experiences toward one career goal. Use either "Experience" or "Professional and Volunteer Experience" as a heading.

   You may, however, decide not to combine the two experiences if you've held paid and volunteer positions at the same time. Trying to list them all together on one time line could make it difficult for the employer to sort out. Also, if your volunteer work is quite different from your paid experience and isn't all that relevant to your career goal, you might be better off listing it separately.

3. **List paid positions only.** If your volunteer experience isn't all that extensive or relevant to your job goal, you can consider listing your activities at the end of the resume in a Memberships and Activities section, or you can simply omit them entirely.

The listing for each position in the Experience section should look something like this:

1998-2001   *Operations Assistant, Replay Records, Indianapolis, IN*
- *Assisted in managing and supervising central warehouse operations, including traffic management and distribution.*
- *Contracted, coordinated, and scheduled freight operations between four stores.*
- *Recommended and implemented new handling procedure, which better protected fragile warehouse inventory.*
- *Assisted in reorganizing warehouse operations and freight distribution, resulting in $75,000 savings annually.*

If you've held several jobs with one company, draw attention to it. Such staying power shows you're a loyal, promotable employee. To avoid repeating the employer's name for each position, and to show your ability to handle increasing responsibilities, you might want to list your positions as shown in the example below.

1989-present	Haverford Barge Company, Cincinnati, OH

Director, 1998-present
Handle profit/loss for $1.5M export facility. Provide general terminal services sales for 12 Midwest river facilities.
- Manage daily merchandising and personnel for Ohio export facility, which has achieved gross sales of more than $40M in last two years, a 45% increase.
- Expanded business by developing new European customers in Spain, France, and Portugal.
- Manage all risk aspects for commodities and negotiate all freight and FOE arrangements.

Sales/Special Projects Manager, 1992-1998
Coordinated all sales work for products other than whole grain at largest river facility.
- Completed contracts with ocean freight companies for bagging contracts and took program to more than 40,000 short tons in one year.
- Developed and directed small fleet of owner/operators to expand business and take advantage of various seasonal trucking opportunities.

Grain Merchandiser, 1989-1992
One of two merchandisers responsible for originating grain on an FOE truck basis in four states.
- Expanded services 17% while reducing budgets 5%.
- Exceeded all first-year forecasts by more than $500,000.

In a chronological format, list your most recent position first and then work backwards. Usually, your first few entries will contain more information than the last few, indicating more extensive experience as you've progressed through your career.

When listing your positions, be sure to include:

❑ Name of employer.

❑ Employer's location.

❑ Dates of employment (or affiliation, if volunteer work).

❑ Position or job title.

❑ A summary of your responsibilities.

❑ Major accomplishments.

You'll want to provide all of this information for the first three or four positions on your resume, or for your first seven to 10 years of experience. For any remaining positions, go into detail only if you have a particular achievement to highlight. Otherwise, just list the employer's name and location, your position and your dates of employment.

Here's a good way to present the elements for each position:

▶ **Employer or organization name and location.** List the company's full name and location. If the organization is better known by its nickname or acronym, use the full name and then follow with the acronym in parentheses. For example: International Business Machines (IBM). After that first reference, you may use the initials.

▶ **Dates of employment.** State the month and year you began and left each position only if you worked primarily short-term jobs (during school, for example). Otherwise, note only the year you joined and left each company (or each new job title within the same company).

▶ **Your job title.** Avoid trying to improve your job status by "creatively enhancing" your job title. Your prospective employer may have another name for such a stretch: he'll term it a lie. Let your job responsibilities and accomplishments, which should immediately follow the job title, do the embellishing for you.

However, if your company uses unusual job titles, such as "group leader" instead of "manager" or "supervisor," it would be okay to list the more common title on your resume. You might want to mention such a change to your former boss so he won't be surprised when contacted for a reference.

▶ **Summary of responsibilities.** Keep it brief, preferably one or two succinct statements. Use broad terms to indicate your level of responsibility and focus on aspects most relevant to the position you're seeking. There's no need to explain to a company that manufacturers dental supplies what a dental supply sales representative does. And don't forget "action" words!

▶ **Major accomplishments.** Here's your chance to show the employer you were successful in each former position. State your accomplishments, if possible, in quantitative terms: how much money you saved the company annually or the percentage you increased sales. Be specific and, again, use action words. If you're having trouble, refer back to Chapter 1, where developing this section is discussed at length.

Education

Information about your education generally follows the Experience section. However, your educational background should come *first* if you are:

▶ A recent college graduate with little job experience.

▶ Changing careers and your education is more relevant to your new career than your most recent job experience.

▶ Seeking a job for which specialized education is a prerequisite for employment.

The Education section usually features only basic information, including the name and location of the school, date of graduation, degree or major area of study, and GPA (optional).

List only your most recent degree, unless you want to list both your Bachelor's and Master's degrees (particularly if they are in different areas, such as a Bachelor's degree in management and a Master's degree in marketing). If you have a college degree, employers assume you graduated from high school, so omit that high school listing and use the space for more important information that sells you and your qualifications.

When stating college and trade-school degrees, you can use abbreviations (B.S., B.A., M.B.A.) or spell them out (Bachelor of Arts). It doesn't matter—just be consistent.

If you want to emphasize your degree, put it first in the entry, followed by the school information, like this:

Bachelor of Science in Computer Science, 1993, Eastern Montana University, Elkville

Note that because the state's name is part of the university's name, there's no need to repeat it.

If you graduated from a well-known and well-respected college, you may want to put the college first, like this:

Harvard University, Cambridge, MA, B.S. in Business Management, Cum Laude, *1999*

If you've had any extraordinary educational experiences—foreign exchange, a seminar with a famous professor, a research assistant position—include them on your resume to demonstrate that you are someone who is "more than ordinary," who accepts new and unusual challenges and has been recognized for excellence:

B.A. English, Babcock College, Lincoln, NB, 1998
  • *Award for excellence for participation in E.L. Doctorow seminar*
  • *One year of foreign study at Birmingham (England) University*

For guidance on handling special situations—if you didn't graduate from college, had a less-than-spectacular GPA or you're changing careers—refer back to Chapter 1.

List details of your high school education only if you are a recent graduate or did not attend college or trade school. If you earned a GED, list when and where you received it. A typical high school listing would look like this:

Carthidge High School, Carthidge, WI, graduated May 1989

If you attended more than one high school, list only the one from which you received your diploma.

You might consider listing a few school courses if they're relevant to the job you're seeking and you have no job experience. But don't get carried away—only include those most relevant to the position you're seeking.

If you've been out of high school several years, there's really no need to list such information at all. By now, you've probably got some solid job experience, and that will interest an employer much more than your high school education.

Licensing, certification, and special skills/training

After you detail your education, you'll want to feature any special training or licensing. If you'd rather, you can include this information in the Education section.

Indicate any special training you've had and any professional licenses or certification you possess. Your heading will vary depending on the information included. Some suggestions: "Professional Licenses," "Certifications," "Professional Training" or "Special Training."

Remember to include:

❑ Name and type of license.

❑ State or states in which it is valid.

❑ Date license/certification acquired.

❑ Number of license, if appropriate.

For example:

New York City Teaching Certification, special education, 1997
New Mexico Real Estate License, 2002
New Jersey Plumbers License 2386

For special training, include:

❑ Name of the course.

❑ Name and location of the institution at which it was given.

❑ Date you completed the training.

Details about extensive, special training—not just half- or full-day seminars— deserve inclusion, perhaps even highlighting, on your resume. The information can be presented like this:

Telephone Central Office Design: Completed intensive, 3-month training
program. New Jersey Bell Research Center, Bell Mead, NJ, June 1999

Military experience

Don't forget to profile your military experience, including special training and accomplishments. Here's a sample listing:

2000-2002	Air Force Flight Test Center, Samuels Air Force Base, FL
	Prepared technical and safety flight test plans, reviewed and approved technical reports and authorized specific flight profiles.
	• Directed more than 150 hazardous, low-level flight programs with no safety incidents.
	• Created published standards of radar altimeter suitability as test data source.
	• Implemented computerized database to control aircraft software configuration.

Memberships and activities

One of the last sections on your resume may cover your outside interests. If you choose to include it, the title you give this section should communicate its content, such as "Professional Affiliations," "Community Activities," or "Memberships and Activities." If you belong to several organizations or have several outside activities, list only those you feel would mean the most to prospective employers (if you include any at all).

Awards and honors

If you've received any special recognition related to your work, you should mention that honor in your Experience section. However, if you have some other award or honor that you think would be meaningful to an employer, list it here. Just remember, the hiring manager may never get to this part of your resume, so don't expect to "wow" her here—do it earlier! Here are two examples:

> *Outstanding Contribution Award, Boy Scouts of America, 2000*
> *Performance Award, Montclair Theater, NJ, 1998*

What if you've gotten off to a bad start and haven't worked six months at any one job? Or you've stayed home a few years to raise children and now are ready to reenter the work force? Or recently graduated from school and have little or no job experience? Or are radically changing your career focus?

Then you may need to consider a functional resume.

The functional format

If you don't have a stable work history or have changed careers in midstream, the functional resume may present your experience and accomplishments in the best light. A standard functional resume would include the following elements:

- ❑ Name header.
- ❑ Objective (optional).
- ❑ Qualification summary or profile (optional but usual).
- ❑ Skills and achievements by area.
- ❑ Employment (listing only).
- ❑ Education (listing only).
- ❑ Other (Military service, Awards, Professional Affiliations, Memberships, Activities, Publications, as appropriate).

With a functional resume, your qualifications, experience, and achievements are grouped into "skill areas," rather than tied to specific positions and dates. How you group your qualifications depends on your career direction, but possible headings include:

- ▶ Communication skills.
- ▶ Leadership skills.

▸ Customer service experience.

▸ Organizational skills.

▸ Technical experience.

▸ Sales experience.

▸ Management experience.

▸ Financial skills.

▸ Teaching/training skills.

You may also use a "catchall" heading such as "Career Profile," "Management Profile," "Executive Profile," or "Professional Skills Profile," under which skill "key words" can be included.

In a functional resume, emphasis is placed on *what* you've achieved, not where and when you achieved it. The idea is to highlight your skills in particular areas. List skills in their order of importance or marketability, with the most important first. Include two or more specific achievements from your previous work, volunteer, or educational experiences to illustrate your mastery of each skill.

Because most employers are not as familiar with the functional resume, some may suspect that a prospective employee who uses it is trying to hide something. However, you should seriously consider the functional format if:

▸ Your work history doesn't exactly match your new career goals.

▸ You don't have a great deal of experience related to the position for which you're applying.

▸ You have noticeable gaps in your work history.

Most elements of the functional resume are handled in the same manner as a chronological resume, except for work experience and accomplishments. Instead of listing each position you've held on a detailed time line, you'll profile your experience and accomplishments according to areas of skill.

Objective and summary of skills

Employers may have trouble determining your career or job goal from a functional resume, so it's a good idea to include a Job Objective or Skills Summary.

Present your information as you would if writing a chronological resume (see that section earlier in this chapter).

Skill and experience profile

Divide your experience into general areas of skill, and briefly state experience, qualifications, and accomplishments related to each area.

To determine which skill areas to highlight, consider what the prospective employer needs for the position you're seeking. Your experience can come from paid positions, volunteer work, school courses, even at-home responsibilities, such as controlling the household budget.

Under each skill heading, list four or five experiences or accomplishments. The sample below profiles a woman with no paid job experience who is seeking a position as a food service manager. Note how she has selected skill categories relevant to such a position (management skills, budgeting skills) and has strong volunteer and in-home experience to support her qualifications.

Organizational/management skills
- For 10 years, organized, hosted, planned menu, and supervised preparation of all food for 300 guests at annual cattle association picnic.
- Organized up to 120 volunteers and supervised food service and forecasting for State Fair beef tent, raising $100,000 annually for state association.
- Chaired meal portion of home economics club's annual fall bazaar/luncheon, including purchasing goods and supervising food preparation.
- Organized and supervised up to 25 volunteers for sorority's annual Fall craft sale.

Financial budgeting skills
- Skilled in handling computerized bookkeeping for 1,200-acre grain and 250-head cattle-farming operation.
- Initiated and completed data entry from manual to computerized record-keeping system, reducing bookkeeping time and improving account analysis.
- Experienced in monthly business and household budgeting and timely payment of personal and business accounts.
- Consistently brought food purchases in under budget and increased net gain for a variety of organizations.

Special dietary experience
- Experienced in planning and creating low-fat, low-sugar, and low-sodium meals.
- Skilled in presenting knowledgeable instruction on proper food handling and storage.

Even relatively modest experience can be made to appear more impressive using a functional format:

Childcare Experience
- Provided in-home day care for six preschoolers for five years.
- Assisted with toddler care in corporate day-care center.
- Developed "child file" system that made vital medical data easier to access and maintain.

Management Experience
- Supervised three cashiers as first-line supervisor in large discount store.
- Created employee scheduling procedure that resolved long-standing staffing conflict.
- Named Employee of the Month for designing and implementing improved inventory-return system.

Using a time line

While some other resume books contend it's not necessary to include specific dates for your employment or volunteer experience in a functional resume, omitting such information may make prospective employers suspicious. It certainly makes it more difficult for them to cull the information they want. And why would you want to make it more difficult for them to do *anything*?

Your entries can be brief, but you're smart to include dates. Present each job in chronological order, such as the following:

> **WORK HISTORY**
> - Assistant farm manager and bookkeeper, Raleigh, Ohio, 1985-present
> - President, Raleigh County Home Economics Club, Raleigh, Ohio, 1990-present
> - Food manager, Ohio Cattle Association, Columbus, Ohio, 1990-1999

Other elements

All other elements of the functional resume follow the guidelines established for chronological resumes earlier in this chapter.

The combination format

One way to overcome employer objections to the functional resume and still position yourself in the most positive light is to use a combination format—melding the safety of a chronological structure and the impact of a skills-based functional approach. By focusing first on your most marketable skills in a Career or Executive Profile, you get the immediate impact of the functional resume. By then resorting to a normal chronological listing of your work experience, you give employers what *they* want—a clear step-by-step picture of your employment history.

Using a combination format can also be a practical consideration. If you are considering a number of positions for which entirely different skills should be emphasized, you can easily redraft the "Profile" section for each new position without having to alter the majority of your resume—the information in the chronological portion could remain unchanged.

Here's the order for a combination resume:

❑ Name header.

❑ Objective (optional).

❑ Summary of Qualifications or "Profile" (optional).

❑ Skills/Achievements.

❑ Work Experience/Employment.

❑ Education.

❑ Other (Military service, Awards, Professional Affiliations, Memberships, Activities, Publications, Particular skills, as appropriate).

Electronic resumes and online job searches

The biggest change in the job-search process during the last decade is the growth of Internet job-search and resume-posting sites and the use of technology by employers to manage the ever-growing pile of resumes from unwanted (unqualified) candidates.

More large- and medium-sized companies (more than three quarters, according to one study) are having computers scan and sort the thousands of resumes they receive each week by "key words." In general, the more key words the computer detects, the better your chances of making it through the first round of cuts.

What's a key word? It may be a job title, educational degree, skill, number (years of experience, years of management), product, software program or other identifier that defines the requisites of a particular job at a particular company. They are almost exclusively nouns or adjectives, rarely verbs.

How will you know if your resume will be scanned electronically? You won't, but should probably assume it will. So you need to load up on key words, starting with those that appear in the company's job description and advertisements.

Whatever their format, electronic resumes require a slightly different approach than the traditional written kind. Here's what to keep in mind:

▶ Computers don't read cover letters. Your electronic resume has to do the selling job of both.

▶ Length isn't as important. It's okay to go to two, three, even four pages, all the more space for those key words. But be careful: Sooner or later, a real human being will actually look at what you sent.

▶ Computers don't like fancy graphics or unusual fonts (but, then, neither do most recruiters). They may even cause your resume to become "unreadable," which is not a desired outcome. (And unlike paper resumes, for which I recommend a serif font, computers tend to prefer sans-serif fonts.)

▶ Design a key-word resume solely for online and e-mail use. That way, you can design it to be computer-friendly, emphasizing key words, eliminating italics and boldface, using a different font.

It's impossible to include a detailed discussion of electronic resumes in this book. Luckily, it's also unnecessary, since I can refer you to Rebecca Smith's *Electronic Resumes and Online Networking, 2nd Edition* (Career Press, 2000), which will tell you absolutely everything else you need to know about preparing resumes for e-mailing, sending them via an electronic form, or posting them on a Website. (Be aware that the vast majority of resume-posting Internet sites now have software that allows you to recreate your resume on their site simply by following a form. The days of needing to learn HTML are long gone.)

Some things remain the same

Whatever format you choose, remember these essential factors as you construct your resume:

▶ Put your best foot forward. Your resume is your professional calling card, your "Here I Am!" advertisement. Show prospective employers how you can address their specific needs, that you have the goods and can deliver. Emphasize the experience and qualifications that are most relevant to the positions you're seeking. If you have more than one career goal, you'll need to create a slightly different resume for each.

▶ Make every word count. Be clear and concise. Your resume will probably get only 30 seconds of attention, so focus on the information that best illustrates your qualifications and sets you apart from the crowd.

▶ Don't use wishy-washy, vague terms. Give your resume power with action words (see page 40).

▶ Make sure your resume isn't a giant job description, but rather a tightly written history of your job experiences and *accomplishments*.

▶ Forget the showy, flowery or creative approach. Impress employers with your ability to communicate clearly and effectively with simple language in concise phrases.

Length, words, and punctuation

For the vast majority of you, your resume should be no longer than two pages. Employers won't read any more than that, anyway. If you can fit your resume onto one page, that's fine—don't stretch it to two thinking it will appear more impressive. Among other qualities, employers are looking for organizational and communication skills. If you can't sum up your qualifications in two pages or less, they'll pass you by. (The possible exceptions: executives at the very top of the food chain and those with an extensive list of publications and speaking engagements.)

As discussed in Chapter 1, use words with "punch"—action words that carry an impact. For help, see the sample list of such words on page 40.

Use those action words to begin tightly written phrases—your entries don't need to be full sentences. In fact, it's best if they're not—it keeps you from getting wordy.

Leave out unnecessary articles, such as "I," "an," and "the."

And finally, don't get too hung up on punctuation. Whether you write "October, 1994" or "October 1994" isn't all that critical—just be consistent.

Action words

Use any of the following action words to add
impact and energy to your resume:

accomplished	enlarged	planned
achieved	established	prepared
adjusted	evaluated	presided
administered	examined	processed
advised	expanded	produced
analyzed	flagged	programmed
approved	formulated	projected
arranged	founded	promoted
assisted	gathered	proposed
budgeted	generated	provided
built	guided	purchased
calculated	headed	recommended
charted	identified	reduced
compared	implemented	referred
compiled	improved	regulated
completed	increased	reorganized
composed	initiated	replaced
conducted	inspected	reported
consolidated	installed	represented
constructed	instituted	researched
consulted	instructed	restored
controlled	integrated	reviewed
conceptualized	interpreted	revised
coordinated	invented	scheduled
counseled	justified	selected
created	lectured	served
decreased	led	sold
delivered	lobbied	solved
designated	maintained	studied
designed	managed	supervised
detected	modified	supplied
determined	motivated	systematized
developed	negotiated	taught
devised	obtained	tested
diagnosed	operated	traced
directed	ordered	trained
discovered	organized	translated
distributed	overhauled	updated
edited	performed	utilized
eliminated	persuaded	won
		wrote

Things to forget

You may have noticed there's been no discussion about photos, personal statistics, or job references. That's because *they don't belong on a resume*. Here are all of the elements you should *omit* from your resume:

▶ **The heading "RESUME."** Employers know a resume when they see one. Don't waste space by stating the obvious. Allow yourself an extra line for shameless self-promotion.

▶ **Why you left past jobs.** Even if there were *positive* reasons—a promotion, transfer, or being spirited away by the competition—this is the kind of detail to trot out during your interview, not put on your resume. As for the negative possibilities—disciplinary problems, layoffs, outright firings—you wouldn't even *think* of including them, would you? I didn't expect so.

▶ **Job references.** Wait until the employer asks for references before you provide them. Of course, you should have them handy on a separate sheet. Just don't automatically include them with your resume. And, since most employers will presume that your "references" are "available on request," you needn't include that phrase at the bottom of your resume, either.

However, if one of your references is someone known to or respected by the employer, you could attach a separate sheet with his or her address and phone number.

Make sure every reference on your list is aware he or she may receive a phone call...and is fully prepared to swear you are as close to divinity as any human could be.

▶ **Salary information.** Providing salary information—either your "history" or "requirements"—allows a prospective employer to eliminate you from consideration (you're too expensive) or determine how little he can get away with paying you. Don't include it on your resume.

A better way to address the situation is to mention in your cover letter that you will be happy to discuss your salary requirements when you have a better idea of what the job entails. But avoid discussing salary at all until the prospective employer mentions it! There is absolutely nothing to be gained by bringing it up first.

▶ **Personal statistics.** Details of your personal life aren't important to your ability to perform the job, so leave them out. What does the fact that you're 6'4" and married have to do with managing a record store? It's considered unprofessional to include such information.

▶ **Photos.** Unless required by your profession (actor, model, broadcast journalist, etc.) *don't* include a photo. Many employers, to avoid potential discrimination, will remove the picture before circulating the resume, anyway.

41

▶ **Personality profiles.** Hiring professionals agree that statements such as "hard working," "team player" and "dedicated" are ignored because they are biased. So leave out your personal attributes and let your experience *prove* that you're "hard working," "a team player," and "dedicated."

▶ **Feelings about travel and/or relocation.** If they are positive, you may mention them in a cover letter, especially if one or both have been listed as requirements for the job. If you are anti-travel and dead-set against relocating, why are you applying for a job that requires both?

▶ **Testimonials.** Testimonials—endorsements from former employers—don't belong on a resume. Let your accomplishments and experiences speak for themselves. If you have a testimonial on the writer's company letterhead, you can attach it to your resume, if you wish. Just realize it could be construed as biased and, therefore, ignored.

Remember: You're only working on a rough draft of your resume, so don't demand perfection just yet. Mull things over, make changes, and when you think you're ready to move on, read Chapter 3 to learn how to design a resume that almost screams "Read *Me!*"

DESIGNING AND EDITING YOUR PERFECT RESUME

Imagine your resume sitting on a hiring manager's desk. Have you made it inviting to look at, with plenty of white space, a neat and clean appearance, and an easy-to-read typeface?

Bingo! First impressions are important. You may have achieved 250 percent of your sales goal for a Fortune 500 company, but if your skills and accomplishments are poorly presented, no one's even going to notice them.

You've gone to an awful lot of time and trouble to carefully organize your information, select an appropriate format, and anguish over effective wording. You surely don't want all that hard work to go to waste just because of a lousy presentation.

Want to make a good first impression? Looking for a professional presentation? Your strategy is simple:

▶ Make it easy to read.

▶ Use lots of white space.

▶ Make it neat.

▶ Make it clean.

In addition, although you won't have "RESUME" tattooed across the top of the page, your product should *look* like a resume. Several job hunters have come up with clever ideas that get them noticed...but nothing else. Gimmicks rarely work. When preparing your resume, it's best to be businesslike and professional.

So, how do you make a good first impression with your resume? Try these 19 tips:

19 tips to a great-looking resume

1. **Limit your resume to one or two pages.** Two-page resumes are quite acceptable, even for first-time job seekers. It's understood that if you've been working for several years, you may need two pages to fully document your experience and accomplishments. Don't cut out vital information just to get your resume down to one page, but never go more than two pages.

2. **Emphasize quality over quantity**. If your pages look too cluttered, you need to do a little editing and focus on the information that's most relevant to your chosen field. Reducing type size, shrinking margins, and closing up spaces isn't the way to do it. A crowded look is overwhelming and uninviting.

3. **If you have a two-page resume, put your name and "page 2" at the top of the second page.** If your pages happen to become separated—not an uncommon occurrence—someone will (hopefully) notice and (hopefully) reattach them.

4. **Use a serif typeface**—the kind with the little "doodads" on all the letters. Tests have proven serif type is easier on the eye...and therefore, easier to read. Serif typefaces include New Century Schoolbook, Palatino, Bookman, Times, Courier, and Souvenir.

   This typeface is Helvetica. It's a sans-serif style.
   Don't use it.

5. **Stick to traditional typefaces.** Stay away from the fancy or cutesy ones.

6. **Select a readable size.** Never use anything smaller than 10-point type for the body of your resume. You may go up to 12 points. Your header can be even larger—typically two or more points larger than your body type.

7. **Don't mix typefaces.** Resist the urge to play with typefaces. Pick one and stick with it. When an amateur tries to do a little "designing," the result is inevitably...amateurish.

8. **Highlight with boldface type.** Boldface type is the darker, heavier type that leads off each of the entries on this page. Using boldface type can help you emphasize certain elements of your resume and draw attention to them.

   For example, you might want to boldface your name, job titles, the names of employers, and your degree. These elements would then stand out as a recruiter glances over your resume. However, don't get too carried away, or you'll lose the effect. (And be careful to eliminate boldface from your electronic resume.)

9. **Use ALL CAPS and underlining sparingly, if at all**. Don't underline words or phrases in your body copy. Research shows that underlining and capitalizing whole words slows and even stops the eye while reading. Save these treatments for your name header and section heads. (And, again, eliminate them from an electronic resume.)

10. **Avoid *italic* type.** Italic type often is used in publications to emphasize a word or phrase, but don't do it in your body copy. First of all, it just adds another type style, which is something you want to avoid. In addition, your goal in

writing your resume is to emphasize everything through clear, concise phrases. Italics would only be redundant and could actually detract, as italic type is harder to read. (One exception: I like using italic type for college honors— *cum laude, with honors, with distinction,* etc.

11. **Use generous margins.** Leave at least a one-inch margin at the top of the page and, if possible, one-inch borders around the other three sides. Never use less than a half-inch border. Wide margins create a pleasant, uncluttered look.

12. **Use "ragged right" layout.** Don't worry about "justifying" or "evening up" your right margin, such as the right margins in this book. (Notice how all of the lines end at exactly the same point.) Instead, just let the lines end where they may, as in the following example:

    This paragraph uses a ragged right style. Notice how the uneven line breaks create attractive white space around the edges. A justified paragraph looks "boxy" and places needed white space between words instead of at the end of the lines.

13. **Avoid hyphens.** Hyphens break up words and, consequently, the flow of a hiring manager's eyes as she reads about your qualifications and exploits.

14. **Single-space between lines of each listing.** And double-space between sections and paragraphs. This approach breaks up body copy and creates an attractive, balanced look.

15. **Use bullets to highlight accomplishments.** Key points can get lost in a paragraph format. Using bullets helps organize information in digestible pieces and works to emphasize those key points. Look at the following examples— you'll notice the difference immediately:

    Military Personnel Management Officer, Arizona Air National Guard, Midway Field, AZ
    Administered and managed personnel function for staff of 26. Increased office-support capabilities and decreased required overtime by 50%. Initiated new mail procedures and streamlined and standardized routing forms and procedures, which improved work flow and reduced "lag" time. As central coordinator for Headquarters' enlisted members, designed programs that led to documented increases in performance, production and morale.

    Military Personnel Management Officer, Arizona Air National Guard, Midway Field, AZ
    Administered and managed personnel function for staff of 26.
    - Increased office-support capabilities and decreased required overtime by 50%.
    - Initiated new mail procedures and streamlined and standardized routing forms and procedures, which improved work flow and reduced "lag" time.
    - As central coordinator for headquarters' enlisted members, designed programs that led to documented increases in performance, production, and morale.

16. **Keep bulleted items to two or three lines of copy.** The whole idea of using bullets is to provide information in short bursts. When you start getting windy, bullets lose their effect.

17. **Keep paragraph length to no more than four or five lines.** Otherwise your reader will give up trying to wade through the sea of information.

18. **Shorten your line length.** Studies have shown the easiest copy to read is that which asks your eyes to travel just a short distance back and forth across the page. To keep your line length short, consider indenting all body copy about two inches from the left margin and put only section heads and accompanying dates to the left. You can find a number of resumes that effectively use this format among the samples that follow.

19. **Find the look that fits you.** There are 101 sample resumes in a variety of styles starting on page 60. Find one you like, modify it as necessary...and create the resume that reflects *you*.

Editing your resume

Now that you've roughed out your resume, have it in some semblance of order, and have applied these 19 tips, it's time to put it on the chopping block and trim the excess fat.

What? You think it's pretty good? Well, maybe it is. But it never hurts to do a little fine tuning. You want a professional product, one that shows you've spent time and thoughtful consideration putting it together, don't you? You've got to be sure you've communicated your value and worth in an effective, attractive format. You need to look at three areas:

1. The big questions (overall effect).

2. The little questions (details).

3. The proofing (typos and grammar).

The "big" questions

When you first started organizing the information for your resume, you determined what should be included and what shouldn't. Well, it's time to do it again. Here are some questions to ask yourself as you look over your almost-finished product:

Have I shown prospective employers I can fill a need?

Your resume should not be a lengthy job description. Have you told the employers what you can do for *them*...right now? Have you communicated your worth and benefit through results-oriented accomplishments? Have you detailed your achievements?

Have I chosen the right format?

Does your functional format look like you're trying to hide something? Does your chronological format make you look like a job-hopper? Make sure you've highlighted your strengths and avoided raising questions you won't be there to answer.

Have I emphasized my strengths?

And downplayed your weaknesses? There may be problems you have to solve, weaknesses you have to admit, decisions and choices you have to defend—just not on your resume! Again, make sure how you've phrased or formatted specific information doesn't automatically raise questions you really don't want to answer just yet.

Is my resume too long or too cluttered?

Stand back. Hold your resume up. Is it a cluttered jumble of words and lines? Have you left adequate margins? Is it longer than two pages? Trim that fat. Your result will be a tightly written, more attractive, more effective resume.

Does every element count?

Is your Job Objective meaningful and targeted or as exciting as the 14th rerun of *The Sound of Music*? Does your resume say more about you and what you want than how you can benefit an employer? Does your Summary include experience specifically related to your chosen job or career? Do all those memberships you listed really mean anything to an employer? If not, eliminate them. Don't waste valuable space on elements that don't communicate your value or accomplishments.

This would be a good time to show your resume to friends, family, or co-workers to see what suggestions they might have. They'll be much more objective and might even come up with a few skills or achievements you missed.

The little questions

Once you've asked yourself those "big" questions and feel you've sufficiently addressed them, it's time to examine the details. Here's a checklist to guide you through the process:

Name header

❑ Are your name, address, phone number and e-mail address (or other pertinent contact information) clearly displayed at the top of the page?

❑ Did you use the most professional sounding form of your name (Jennifer, not Jenny; William, not Billy)?

❑ Is your address correct? If you're moving soon, did you indicate your future address and the date you'll be there?

❑ Did you list a phone number where you can be easily and reliably reached or where a message can always be left? Did you include an area code? Did you transpose any numbers?

Job objective

❑ Is it focused and precise, stating exactly the position you want?

❑ Is it stated in 12 words or less?

❑ Does it mesh with the rest of your resume? Is it supported by the data you've included about your education, skills, and experience?

❑ Does it exclude you from other positions you might be interested in? If so, should you draft an alternative version with a slightly less-targeted objective (or eliminate it entirely)?

Skills summary

❑ Is it targeted to the job you're seeking?

❑ Does it highlight the qualifications and experience that are most important to *this* prospective employer?

❑ Is it short and concise (two or three brief sentences or four or five bulleted points)?

❑ Have you placed your most relevant qualifications first?

Experience

For chronological resumes:

❑ Did you include the correct starting and ending dates (usually year only) for each position?

❑ Did you use your correct job title or a revised title that accurately reflects your responsibilities and duties?

❑ Did you include the correct name and location of each employer and organization?

❑ Did you limit your job descriptions to short, punchy sentences?

❑ Are any paragraphs longer than five lines? Any bulleted items longer than three lines?

For functional and combination resumes:

❑ Did you use the skill categories most relevant to the job you want?

❑ Did you use business-like terms for category headings (management, organizational, instructional)?

❑ Did you include a brief chronological listing of your work experience at the end of your resume?

For all resume formats:

❏ Did you use strong action words to describe your contributions and achievements?

❏ Did you eliminate "I," "the," and "an" from your body copy?

❏ Did you overuse any particular words?

❏ Did you use acronyms, initials or unfamiliar terms that might not be understood or be misunderstood?

❏ Did you quantify your accomplishments rather than just describe them? For example, did you talk about the money you saved, expenses you cut, percent you increased sales?

❏ If you listed an award, did you explain why you were honored? Did you use the correct name and date for the award? Correctly identify the organization that gave it to you?

Education

❏ Did you check and correctly state the dates you earned your degree(s) or attended particular schools?

❏ Did you verify the type of degree earned and list the correct location of the school from which you earned it?

❏ Did you verify data related to certifications, licenses and other training?

Miscellaneous

❏ Did you include personal references? Pictures? Salary information? Personality traits? The heading "RESUME"? Omit them!

❏ If you listed memberships in various organizations, did you check the spelling of each organization?

Style

❏ Did you leave a one-inch margin at the top and no less than half-inch borders on all other sides?

❏ Did you use at least a 10-point type size?

❏ Did you use a serif typeface?

❏ Did you use capitals or underlining sparingly, if at all?

❏ Did you use boldface type sparingly but wisely? Are the words you emphasized the ones you *want* an employer to notice first?

❏ Did you use a ragged-right margin?

❏ Did you break up large blocks of copy with appropriate line spacing?

❑ Did you use bullets to emphasize specific points within listings?

❑ If your resume is two pages, did you put your name and "page 2" at the top of the second page?

❑ Did you use a consistent style throughout?

Proofreading

Getting a little trying, isn't it? This editing process may be tedious, but it's essential to craft an effective resume. You've put too much effort into your resume at this point to cut any corners. Don't take the chance of having it tossed out by a prospective employer because you spelled "achieved" wrong or used "1938" instead of "1983." Here are some tips to help you pick out those errors:

▶ If you're working on a computer, **use your spell-check** program to catch misspelled words. Not all such programs however, will find mis-*used* words, such as *you're* instead of *your*. You may have to detect those yourself.

▶ **Read your resume out loud**. It will help you find typos and misspelled words, awkward sentence structure and repetitive words.

▶ **Get out a ruler** and go through your resume one line at a time. This will force you to slow down your reading and focus more on the words.

▶ **Read from the bottom up**...and backwards. Start in the lower right-hand corner and move toward the top of the page. You won't be able to focus on anything but the words, one by one.

▶ **Ask for help**. Get several people to look over your resume. The more eyes, the better.

Don't give up until you're sure your resume is perfect. When you are sure, proof it again. Then once more.

A few production tips

Now that you've come this far, don't skimp on looks. If you don't have a computer, type your resume on an office-quality typewriter and have it scanned at your local print shop. You can then work with them to choose particular fonts and layouts. Make sure you get a final version of your resume on a computer disk. When you need to update it, you can take it virtually anywhere and have it reprinted.

Here are a few other considerations:

▶ Avoid copy machines. They just don't provide the quality you're looking for. You'll inevitably end up with smudges, streaks, and lines. Use a print shop and get quality results.

▶ Select white, off-white, ivory or buff colored paper. And use black ink. This combination provides excellent contrast and ensures easy readability. (You can cheat a little and use deep blue or even dark brown ink, but now is not the time to see what hot pink ink would look like printed on canary-yellow paper!)

▶ Choose a good-quality, medium weight paper, preferably 24-pound stock or better.

▶ Select a paper stock with a conservative finish. Avoid glossy magazine stock.

▶ Make sure matching stationery (for your cover letters) and envelopes are available to complete your professional look. Print your return address on the envelope and a nice heading on the stationery using a typeface compatible with your resume. Don't over-design it or include pictures or illustrations.

▶ Package each mailing carefully to ensure that what you sent gets there in pristine condition. Over the years, I have received resumes with cigarette burns, resumes stained by juices I didn't care to identify, even resumes that appeared to have taken a long tour of the Bronx Zoo...cage by cage. Don't be labeled a slob just because you wouldn't shell out the extra cash for an overnight delivery service.

Some final thoughts

Your resume isn't cast in stone. Actually, it's a fairly flexible body of work that should change and grow with you.

You never know what tomorrow may bring. Someone in your network may call and tell you your dream job just opened at KLM Company. The position isn't being publicized, they're hiring soon, and you need to get your resume over there right away. If you have to rework your resume, have a typist make corrections, and dash it off it to the print shop before you can send it out, you'll lose valuable time...and maybe a chance to interview for your dream job.

In addition, there are no guarantees in today's job market. Reorganizations and layoffs abound. It's best to adopt the wise scout motto: "Always be prepared."

Your personal life may suddenly change, too. Suppose your spouse is laid off, and you need to go back to work. Or some unforeseen, long-term medical expenses arise and your family needs a second income immediately. During such a stressful time, the last thing you need to be dealing with is writing your resume. Wouldn't it be a relief to know you could go right to your file cabinet and pull out a professional-looking, current resume that effectively communicates your qualifications and achievements?

So keep it current. As soon as you get a new job, earn a degree, complete special training, or achieve a significant goal, get it on your resume.

The remainder of this book includes 101 sample resumes, which cover various personal situations and careers. The resumes are arranged in a variety of formats and are preceded by brief paragraphs that emphasize the strong points in the resumes.

Because this book is not standard paper size (8½" x 11"), all of the resumes have been reduced to fit the book's slightly smaller page size. Please note margins for resumes in this book may not necessarily be one-inch, and typefaces may not be 10-point. However, you still should follow the guidelines established in this chapter under the section, "19 tips to a great-looking resume."

Let's look at 101 resumes that stand out from the crowd...and will ensure you do, too.

GREAT SITUATIONAL RESUMES

4

I commend you for wading through three chapters of my advice when all you *really* wanted was to head straight for the resumes and find one you could adapt for yourself! Well, here they are—101 great resumes that would make any hiring manager stop, look, and...read.

Sample resumes are divided into two general groups. In this chapter are 35 resumes grouped by particular life situations, from seeking a job right after high school to diving back into the work force after raising a family. Chapter 5 features 66 resumes that represent a variety of occupations, from accountant to writer.

Remember: There is no single right way to structure a resume—you can adapt one of the samples that follow or combine a few to create your own unique approach. Review the comments about the resumes on the following pages, examine the resumes themselves—and with what you've learned already, you should have the tools and knowledge to create your own great job-winning resume!

Recent high school graduate *with* experience   60

A quick glance wouldn't reveal that Christopher just graduated from high school, since that fact doesn't appear until the very end of this well-balanced resume. He uses a functional resume to emphasize the skills and abilities he's developed through work and school activities, quantifies results where possible, and communicates his value as a responsible individual who could succeed in a variety of entry-level positions.

Without inflating his title, duties, or responsibilities, he even manages to make his stint as a stock clerk sound like a stroll through the executive suite, not a trudge down the produce aisle!

Recent high school graduate *without* experience   61

Judy may not have any "real" job experience, but the functional format she chose successfully highlights her many career-related skills—the classes, volunteer work, and vocational accomplishments that ably reflect her capabilities. Including relevant courses, memberships, and awards affiliated with her desired position add to the impact of this well-thought-out resume.

Recent college graduate *with* experience   62-64

Janet has demonstrated her ability to communicate by presenting a clear and concise resume. Her work history lends itself well to a chronological resume, which gives her the opportunity to highlight her career-related achievements and contributions. Her GPA and campus activities only strengthen an already impressive resume—one would never describe her as a "grind," yet she managed to earn impressive grades while spending considerable time on her activities. Her honors and accomplishments are directly related to her chosen field and are, therefore, an important addition to her resume.

Michelle has some job experience, but her education and high GPA are her strong points, so she places her educational credentials before her work experience. She has a specific veterinary interest, which she covers in a short, clear Objective. Note that all of her work experience supports her career goal. Because her internship and stint as a lab technician were brief, she includes the actual months worked at each job.

Recent college graduate *without* experience   65

Terry may have never received a paycheck, but his campus activities and accomplishments show just how valuable an employee he could be. His functional resume communicates his management and sales achievements and leadership abilities. He includes a simple but targeted Objective (and a short list of courses) because his career goal may not be evident from his Skills/Abilities Profile. Terry rightly lists his positions with the newspaper and fraternity house as experience, even though they were non-paid, and quantifies his accomplishments.

Mid-career college graduate   66

After nearly 10 years of changing diapers and wiping runny noses, Bridgette earned an elementary education degree and teaching license to prepare for a mid-career change. Although she has some instructional background and extensive experience as a day-care director, her education is her strong point, so she lists it first. Her career-related volunteer work and additional activities show she's a well-rounded individual who enjoys working with children. As all beginning teachers should, she includes a license-specific Objective and details her student teaching experience (no matter how modest).

Mid-career advanced degree   68

Lori is an accomplished accountant who has gradually developed an interest in sales and marketing. In order to pursue a position as an account manager with her current employer (and enhance her marketability with others, if necessary) she earned an MBA in marketing. Lori correctly highlights this credential by moving the Education section immediately after her Profile, in which she does an excellent job of quantifying her sales achievements and emphasizing her strong customer-relations skills and "go-getter" attitude. She eliminates all other potential sections from her resume in order to emphasize her education and solid experience.

Strong education, weak experience   **69**

After eight years of college and post-graduate work, Emilio finally has his doctorate degree, but little else to support it (except his well-written Profile). Therefore, he lists his education first—including his dissertation and thesis topics, highlighting the fact that both were published, a noteworthy accomplishment. Although his work experience is limited, he has done a good job of summarizing his responsibilities and citing specific achievements.

Strong experience, weak education   **70**

Forced to take a job as a machinist to help defray college expenses, James never left the work place...and never earned his college degree. But his resume clearly demonstrates the steady upward progression of his career—he obviously offers prospective employers solid experience and a proven ability to assume increased responsibilities. To describe his situation in the most positive terms, he details his skills and strong work history first and mentions his limited education only at the end of his resume.

Seeking a career change   **72-75**

If you're pursuing a career change, make sure you don't confuse prospective employers by including irrelevant information or, worse, highlighting it. Note how each of these three career changers establishes a clear Objective and includes a Profile highlighting skills relevant to his or her *new* career goal.

Martin can boast of some noteworthy achievements in the financial area, but he's gone back to school, earned his education degree and is ready to get started as a music teacher. His extensive experience as a tutor, piano instructor and choral director support his career change, so he lists them first. He includes his other employment history, even though it's not relevant to his new career, to show he's dependable and employable. Since Martin has already featured his degree in his skills summary, he saves his Education listing for last.

Melinda always had an interest in designing homes, but a growing family and other demands left little time or money for college. Now that her load has lifted, she's ready to give up the banking career that helped pay the bills and seek a full-time job in home design. She lists her strongest points—pertinent education and awards—first. She further supports her new career goal by highlighting related skills she's developed at school and working part-time for a local builder. Her solid previous work history describes a responsible and contributing employee.

Lisa has also had a successful career with a local bank, but she's ready to try a career in real estate. Her functional resume allows her to correlate her mortgage loan experience with the requirements of a new field. She lists additional training relevant to her new career (of course), and although her college degree *isn't* career-related, it's important to include it.

With same company for long period   **76-77**

Moving through a series of jobs with the same company over a long period of time indicates an individual's ability to continually take on more and greater responsibilities. Her resume must proclaim loudly and clearly that she is a loyal, ambitious and eminently promotable professional.

Both William and Meghan draw attention to their staying power by mentioning it in the very first lines of their Profiles and clearly illustrating how their careers progressed from entry-level to supervisory positions. They both quantify their achievements and detail how they contributed to the success of their organizations.

Combining two careers · 78

Susan is fortunate to be talented in two areas—as a dental assistant and in sales management. Rather than work full-time as a dental assistant and try to sell something part-time, she's attempting to utilize both of her skills in a single career—a dental sales representative. Her resume successfully summarizes both her dental skills and sales achievements and clearly communicates how they would complement each other in her chosen profession.

Entry-level, ready to move up · 79

Teresa's resume clearly and concisely shows she has the experience, qualifications, and skills necessary to assume a position with more responsibility. Boasting a solid background in all aspects of human resources, she successfully presents her results-oriented achievements.

Teresa wants prospective employers to understand she's looking for a management position in a mid-size firm, so she makes that her highly specific Objective. The Summary of Qualifications supports her goal by citing the management skills she's developed—budget planning, forecasting and program administration.

Assistant, ready to move up · 80

In nine years, Monica has advanced from a temporary secretarial employee to a senior administrative assistant, and she isn't finished. To show she's qualified for a management position, she highlights her experience in budget planning, department goal-setting, and program administration and development. Her track record proves that she can assume increased responsibility while posting excellent, quantifiable results. Although she doesn't have a college degree, she lists undergraduate studies in related fields and includes career-related memberships.

Small business owner, ready to move out · 82

Though self-employed, Steven successfully highlights his managerial and organizational skills, business accomplishments, sales talents, and supervisory and budgetary experience, all valuable qualifications for a management position. Notice that he uses an Objective to clarify his career goal and quantifies results wherever possible.

Steven also highlights his international capabilities, citing relevant work projects and noting his proficiency in Spanish. He includes positions held before he started his own business to assure potential employers he has "real" corporate experience.

Difficulties with work history

If your work history includes lots of jobs, lots of careers or lots of moving; long gaps in employment; or real negatives like being fired or laid off, you must focus on the positive aspects of your career and neutralize the glaring negatives. Here are a variety of situations and how to successfully write and design your resume to handle them.

Job hopper   84

Why hasn't Margaret stayed at any job for more than one year? Because she's developed a reputation as a top trouble-shooter who comes in, fixes problems and moves on. As a result of her success, she has been "consistently recruited" (it says so right in her Summary) and has moved more frequently than some employers would like *because each new position was a promotion*. Despite her successful positive spin, Margaret should probably consider eliminating the months from her history—it just draws attention to the problem she has to explain. (I left them in just so I could draw *your* attention to them.)

Career hopper   86

After a varied career in management, sales, and politics, Steven has finally decided to stick with politics. After earning a master's degree in a related field and completing a legislative internship, he's ready to enter the arena. He lists his *new* career-related information first, including a clear Objective, a Skills Profile and his education. His work history, though not related to his new career, is solid, results-oriented, and shows he's a contributor. Note that Steven also has become involved in activities affiliated with his new field, which, of course, he makes sure to include.

False starter   88

Paul has an erratic career history, but he feels he's found his niche in warehouse operations. He's not currently looking for a new position, but he would certainly welcome the move into management if the opportunity presented itself. Although Paul is a job-hopper, he suspects omitting employment dates will just raise suspicions, so he leaves them in. He even draws attention to his job hopping with the first word in his summary—"varied"—as a way of "answering" the objection before it's raised.

By seeking to move up in a field in which he can boast recent accomplishments, he's doing the best he can to own up to his erratic work history while declaring it a thing of the past.

Frequent mover   89

Mark has relocated a lot, but since each move has been a promotion within the same company, it isn't a negative. Mark mentions his general responsibilities and then covers each move independently, noting the outstanding accomplishments that led to his next promotion. His resume is an excellent example of featuring results-oriented accomplishments.

Little training, few skills   90

Anna may not have many skills or much training, but what she does, she does well—she's even earned awards for her work. Anna emphasizes her ability to enhance office operations and get the job done right and on time. Because she has no post-secondary training, she includes information about her high school education.

Fired or laid off   91

Glenn was laid off or fired from a series of jobs before he hit his stride as a courier, and he'd like to stay in that area. He feels strongly about his capabilities and is prepared to answer questions about his somewhat erratic work history, so he uses a chronological resume. He avoids raising suspicions by including all dates.

Reentering the job market after raising children   92

Phyllis has some paid work experience, though she took significant time off to raise her children until they were all in school. Now she's ready to return to full-time teaching. Phyllis doesn't limit her resume to the teaching assignment she held 10 years ago. Doing so would omit the valuable (and career-related) volunteer and instructional experience she's had since. She presents the picture of a well-rounded individual with mature, professional experience, able to manage several responsibilities simultaneously.

Erratic job history due to husband's relocating   94

Gretchen's husband works for a major chemical company and has accepted promotions that have forced frequent family moves. Because she is an excellent employee, Gretchen has always been able to find a position in each new city. She chose a functional resume to emphasize her skills and accomplishments and de-emphasize the number of employers she's had over the last 15 years. Notice how consistently she quantifies her results.

Translating volunteer experience into work skills   95

Anne has never earned a paycheck, but look at the resume she's developed based on her volunteer experience with library, church, school and community service organizations! She uses a functional resume to profile her excellent management and leadership skills and support her career goal. Note her results-oriented listings.

Woman entering traditionally male field   96

Michelle is a mechanical engineer trying to advance in the automotive industry. She's been in the same position for five years now, and she's ready to move into project management. She chose a functional resume to emphasize her skills and downplay the fact she's really had only one job.

Challenges facing older adults

Although it shouldn't be, age discrimination is still a fact of life for many older working adults. If you fall into this category, there are ways to downplay your age but not your valuable contributions or mature experience. Just remember that omitting dates entirely *isn't* one of your options—that approach will only raise suspicions and perhaps make you appear older than you are. The first resume featured in this section offers a unique solution to the "date" dilemma.

No paid job experience   97

Nancy is a recent widow in need of a steady income. While she has a solid and varied volunteer background, her strongest selling point is her catering experience. She put together a functional resume highlighting her excellent management and financial skills—essential qualifications in the food-service business. She deflects guesses about her age by including the number of years with each organization—but not actual dates—and by omitting her graduation date.

Coming out of retirement   98

Marcia successfully uses a functional resume to present her extensive professional experience and downplay her age. By organizing her skills in career-related groupings, she proves she has the experience and qualifications necessary to support her career goal. Notice that she includes employment dates, but not until the end of the resume, after she's hooked the prospective employer and can capitalize on the value of her maturity.

Changing careers   **100**

Mason is secure with his age and feels it will be a benefit in his new career as an insurance agent. His age gives him a greater appreciation of the insurance needs of both young and old clients. Therefore, he includes all appropriate dates. He does, however, omit his first 20 years of employment—the work he did isn't relevant to his new career and is quite outdated. Instead, he includes positions that reflect his management and insurance-related experience.

Recently laid off   **102**

Anthony decided to address the age issue by omitting his first few jobs out of college. Work he performed during those years is irrelevant in today's engineering world, anyway. He also omitted his college graduation date—it was too long ago and definitely "dates" him. What remains is a solid resume with results-oriented information relevant to today's marketplace.

Hasn't worked for a while   **103**

To avoid highlighting the fact that she hasn't worked for several years, Deborah chose a functional resume. Her experience is sorted by skill, which emphasizes her strong organizational and administrative talents. She mentions results-oriented achievements where possible and includes her volunteer work. Deborah saves her job listings for last, as her goal is to profile *what* she's achieved, not *where* and *when* she achieved it.

Transitioning out of the military

Military duty provides excellent experience that can easily translate to the civilian job market...when accomplishments are phrased in nonmilitary terms. If you've served in the military, be careful to state your achievements in laymen's terms.

Entering civilian market in unrelated field   **104**

Sandra's military background has provided her with experience in a variety of areas, but she's chosen to pursue a career in teaching. Therefore, while she could have listed a number of accomplishments under each duty, she only zeros in on instructional and training achievements, supporting her career goal with substitute teaching assignments and other career-related activities.

Entering civilian market in related field   **106**

Edward has excellent aeronautical and supervisory experience that he wants to apply in the civilian work force. His Profile clearly focuses on the management and computer skills that will translate well into the civilian business world. Notice how his noteworthy achievements are quantified and explained in laymen's terms.

CHRISTOPHER MORROW

55 Center Drive • Coatsville, FL • 32310 • (305) 555-9745 • CTMorrow@mailbox.net

SKILLS/ABILITIES

Organizational / Management

- Handled stocking and assisted in managing flow of stock in grocery store.
- Prepared weekly inventory reports and submitted to supervisor.
- Recommended new stocking system that reduced stocking time by four hours a week.
- Served as treasurer of high school RC airplane club for two years.
- Coordinated candy sale fund raiser for RC airplane club, netting $350 in profit.
- Helped plan monthly "flyings" and quarterly meetings.

Customer Relations

- Assisted grocery shoppers in finding products.
- Provided carry-out service.
- Created new customer comment program that increased customer satisfaction by 75%.
- Served 78 customers on neighborhood newspaper route; handled billing and collections.
- Initiated revised billing program for paper route, increasing on-time payments by 30%.

Communication

- Wrote articles about RC airplane club for high school newspaper.

WORK HISTORY

Stock clerk, Superthrift, Maddington, FL (Summers and after school, 2001-present)

Newspaper carrier, *Daily Times,* Coatsville, FL (1999-2001)

EDUCATION

Graduate, Washington High School, Coatsville, FL (2002)

JUDY WATKINS
501 Terrace Lane
Huntsville, TX 77341
(409) 555-6623
Judyw@alo.com

Career goal   A secretarial or administrative assistant position

Summary of skills

Organizational

- Worked with local business to update company's secretarial manual (fulfilled class requirement); helped design new memo format, which simplified formatting and gained company-wide acceptance.
- Created responsibilities manual for volunteers at county hospital, which reduced overlapping duties and increased efficiency.
- Assisted in managing volunteers for outpatient information desk at hospital.

Secretarial

- Experienced in document formatting, proofreading and administrative assistant duties.
- Skilled in MicroSoft Works and Lotus 1-2-3 on IBM compatible system.
- Ability to type 70 words per minute with no errors.

Communication

- Delivered a speech to local civic clubs and philanthropic organizations on the importance of hospital volunteers, which brought in seven new volunteers.
- Wrote articles for local newspaper on vocational team's achievements at district and state contests.

Education   Huntsville High School, Huntsville, TX (GPA - 3.7/4.0)
Graduation expected June 2002

Related course work:
Bookkeeping I & II, Typing, Advanced Typing, Computer Operations, Word Processing I & II, Business Writing, Vocational Business Curriculum (2 years)

Awards   Outstanding High School Volunteer, Warren County Hospital (2002)
State Business Vocations Contest (2001)

- Document formatting (1st)
- Business knowledge (2nd)
- Administrative assistant competition (2nd)

Memberships   Business Professionals of America (student member)
Texas Association of Hospital Volunteers
Junior Rotarian

JANET MEYERS
1635 Elizabeth Drive
Worthington, OH 44203
(614) 555-4987
JLM@mailstar.net

CAREER GOAL   A position as a sports reporter or city reporter for a daily
metropolitan newspaper

SUMMARY OF
QUALIFICATIONS
- Experienced sports writer and editor.
- Strong background in newspaper mechanics, layout and design.
- Skilled in developing and implementing a variety of programs.
- Well-developed organizational and leadership skills.
- Familiarity with city government and how it operates.

PROFESSIONAL
EXPERIENCE
2000-2002

Staff, *The Exponent,* **Purdue University, West Lafayette, IN**
- Served as copy editor, assistant city desk editor and assistant
sports editor for campus newspaper.
- Assigned and covered city stories and sporting events.
- Established "stringer" system among nonrevenue sports, which
resulted in increased coverage of those sports in the newspaper.
- Developed program matching city officials with newspaper
reporters to enhance understanding of city government and its
operations; resulted in more accurate coverage of council
meetings and its decisions.

1999-2002

Feature Writer, Purdue Sports Information Office, West Lafayette, IN
- Developed and implemented hometown feature program, which
increased coverage of Purdue sports in athletes' local newspapers.
- Wrote and placed nearly 50 articles throughout the United States.
- Wrote three articles for the game-day football program.

**PROFESSIONAL
EXPERIENCE (Cont.)**
1996-1998

**Sports Reporter/High School Correspondent, *Daily Record*,
Worthington, OH**
- Covered community and high school sports for local newspaper.
- Assisted with galley proofing and page layout.
- Edited news releases for style and content.

EDUCATION
2002

B.A. in Communications, Purdue University, West Lafayette, IN
- Graduated *With Distinction* (5.8/6.0).
- Earned minors in English and History.
- Completed career-related courses in reporting, editing, ethics in journalism, communication law, newspaper layout and design, photography, radio and television, and magazine article writing.

**CAMPUS
ACTIVITIES**

Purdue University All-American Marching Band
- Served as flag corps co-captain for three years.
- Wrote at least three new routines for the 40-member flag corps each week and scheduled extra practices when necessary.

Alpha Xi Delta National Sorority
- Completed terms as corresponding secretary, editor and choir director for college sorority.
- Won national recognition for scrapbook layout, design and content.
- Contributed quarterly feature and chapter highlights articles to national publication.
- Organized "donate a window" program, encouraging alumni to purchase new windows for the chapter house.

HONORS
- Alpha Lambda Delta Freshman Scholastic Honorary
- Sigma Delta Chi Journalism Honorary
- Skull and Crescent Leadership Honorary
- Worthington Area Panhellenic Scholarship Award (two years)

Michelle Lee • 21 College Ave., Apt. 6A • Lafayette, IN • 46099 • (317) 555-6126 • MLee@alo.net

Objective

Position as a veterinarian with a small animal practice that emphasizes feline medicine and surgery.

Summary of Qualifications

Excellent training and experience in small animal surgery and treatment. Good background in office management and inventory control. Well-developed client relations skills.

Education

DVM, Purdue University School of Veterinary Medicine, West Lafayette, IN (5.7/6.0 GPA) May 2002

Significant clerkship and course work: Clinical Pathology, Ophthalmology/Small Animal Medicine, Small Animal Surgery, Client Relations, Non-Domestic Animal Medicine.

Internship

Lakeside Animal Hospital, Sturgis, MI
July-September 2001

- Performed and assisted with small and large animal surgery.
- Managed office and medical supplies inventory.
- Assisted on farm calls and handled seven after-hours, large-animal emergencies.
- Recommended and implemented new computer software, which enhanced customer service and patient care by providing print-outs related to prescribed medication.

Work Experience

Animal Disease Diagnostic Lab, Purdue University
September 1999-May 2001

- Performed necropsies on a variety of species.

Sturgis Veterinary Clinic, Sturgis, MI
Summers 1999, 2000

- Completed small animal surgery, treatments and radiography.
- Performed clinical lab work and assisted on farm calls.
- Learned to work with clients, answer questions and address concerns.
- Supervised transition from manual to computerized record keeping, resulting in more accurate patient records and an enhanced annual check-up "reminder" program.

Lab Technician, Purdue University
January-August 1998

- Prepared and interpreted histopathology slides.
- Collected bovine blood samples.
- Ran reproductive hormonal assays.
- Implemented new report procedure, which provided clients with more detailed information.

TERRY LAWSON

65 N. Grant St. • Salt Lake City, Utah • 84107 • (801) 555-1331 • TLaw54@mail.net

OBJECTIVE

Entry-level marketing or management position with a medium-sized business

EDUCATION

Bachelor of Science, Business Administration, University of Utah, Salt Lake City
(Expected June 2002)
Major: Management   Minor: Marketing
Related course work: personnel management, business management, business ethics,
business law, macro economics, statistics, marketing and sales.

SKILLS/ABILITIES

Management
- Developed and implemented new fund-raising program for social fraternity, which brought in more than $1,500 for local charity.
- Worked with local and national alumni chapters to coordinate chapter house expansion, including negotiating a construction contract and schedule.
- Organized and communicated to chapter alumni about a house expansion fund-raising program, which to date has brought in enough to cover 50% of expansion costs.
- Managed chapter house finances for two years, including collecting dues and paying bills.
- Carried a full course load while serving as chapter officer and working on campus newspaper advertising staff.

Sales
- Led campus newspaper advertising staff three consecutive years for most advertising dollars generated.
- Organized and implemented advertising promotion, which increased number of advertisers by 45%.

Communication
- Presented monthly financial reports to chapter members and quarterly reports to national headquarters.
- Corresponded with chapter alumni on progress of house expansion and fund raiser.

Leadership
- Served as fraternity president, business manager and social chairman.
- Named to Skull and Crescent National Leadership Honorary.

EXPERIENCE

Advertising Staff, *Utah Extra,* University of Utah, Salt Lake (1998 - present)
Business Manager, Sigma Chi, University of Utah, Salt Lake (2000 - 2001)

BRIDGETTE T. LARSON

52 N. State St.
Stilesville, NH 03472
(603) 555-9232
BTLar@access.net

CAREER OBJECTIVE

To secure a full-time teaching position at the kindergarten to third-grade level

EDUCATION/LICENSING

Bachelor of Science, Early Childhood Education, University of New Hampshire, Bedford (2001)
New Hampshire State License in Elementary Education (2001)

PROFILE

- Extensive background in early childhood care and education.
- Skilled in developing and implementing lesson plans for all areas of a developmentally appropriate curriculum.
- Able to create and initiate hands-on learning experiences.
- Experienced in designing and implementing integrated learning centers.
- Knowledge and confidence to advise and counsel parents on their child's specific cognitive or emotional problems. .
- Skilled day care and business manager.

STUDENT TEACHING

Student Teacher, Bedford Elementary School, Bedford, NH (March-May 2000)
- Developed and implemented lesson plans for all areas of the third-grade curriculum.
- Established activity/reading center, which provided materials for and challenged students who finished class assignments ahead of others.
- Created, graded and recorded academic progress tests.
- Assisted classroom teacher in organizing three field trips.

Student Teacher, Bedford Elementary School, Bedford, NH (February-March 2000)
- Created and implemented lesson plans for 39 kindergarten students during six-week teaching assignment.
- Designed and implemented integrated learning centers on dinosaurs and ocean life.
- Incorporated sand and water table play into the classroom, encouraging hands-on learning.

CURRENT INSTRUCTIONAL EXPERIENCE

Substitute Teacher, Stilesville Community School Corporation, Stilesville, NH (2001-present)
- ➤ Guide students through lesson plans set by teacher.
- ➤ Help students prepare and organize for classroom lessons/activities and hold them accountable for their work.
- ➤ Assist students in reviewing for exams and completing homework assignments.
- ➤ Maintain disciplined academic atmosphere.
- ➤ Created and gained acceptance for Substitute Teacher's Handbook, which details how to handle substitute assignments, answers common questions, and addresses potential classroom problems.

Volunteer Tutor, Bedford Public Library, Bedford, NH (2000-present)
- ➤ Tutor kindergarten through 3rd-grade students in reading.
- ➤ Work with up to four children each month.
- ➤ Assisted in mainstreaming three remedial reading students into regular reading classrooms.

Owner/Administrator/Teacher, Wee Care Day Care/Nursery School, Stilesville, NH (1990-present)
- ➤ Opened to meet the need for quality, developmentally appropriate day care for 2- to 10-year-old children in the community.
- ➤ Expanded in October 1993 to include infants and toddlers.
- ➤ Began nursery school program in September 1995 to address needs for stay-at-home parents.
- ➤ Provide annual day care for up to 75 children, with more than 125 students enrolled in various programs.
- ➤ Offer developmentally appropriate curriculum, including field trips, guest speakers and hands-on learning experiences for all ages.
- ➤ Participate in community events, such as the Fourth of July parade, home basketball games and holiday programs.
- ➤ Manage staff of 12.

ADDITIONAL ACTIVITIES

Sunday School Teacher, St. Joseph Church, Stilesville, NH
Leader, Girl Scout Child Care Project, Stiles County, NH

LORI T. CHILDERS

455 Bennington Circle • Atlanta, GA • 30332 • (404) 555-2003 • Childers906@mail.net

PROFILE

Solid background in financial analysis and marketing, with strong emphasis in telecommunications account management. Consistently exceed sales goals and customer service expectations. Experienced in handling international accounts and in presenting results of consortium operations. Skilled in developing and implementing standardized policies and procedures.

EDUCATION

M.B.A. Marketing, Georgia Tech University, Atlanta, 2001
B.S. Accounting, University of Nebraska, Lincoln, 1990

CAREER HISTORY

1999-present

Gulf Telephone, Large Business Marketing, Atlanta, GA
Corporate Account Manager
- Exceed sales goals each year, including 150% of goal for 2001.
- Manage five-member account team to serve large business customers.
- Consistently earn highest rating in customer service quality surveys.
- Coordinated and responded to complex customer telecommunications requests, resulting in increased sales and customer satisfaction.
- Sold and worked with a variety of Gulf Telephone products and network and integration services, including SMDS, ISDN, video conferencing, routers, CPEs, and multiplexers.
- Closed the largest network integration sale ever, scored a competitive winback from AT&T, and sold an ISDN data network to a major customer with 150 sites.

1995-1999

Gulf Telephone International, Inc., Atlanta, GA
Financial Manager
- Handled financial analysis and reporting of corporate finances, including activities in the Caribbean.
- Managed finances for domestic and international projects.
- Developed and implemented policies and procedures over financial transactions, resulting in standardized reports.
- Coordinated relationships with other Gulf Telephone finance departments, which helped standardize procedures across all operating groups.

1990-1995

Specter, Williams and Ritz, Atlanta, GA
Senior Accountant
- Managed audit team that performed commercial financial statement audits.
- Planned, budgeted and supervised engagements in excess of 800 hours.
- Developed and implemented client service program, which expanded small-to-medium client base 35%.
- Served government contractors and other commercial customers.

Emilio Sanchez

32 Westview Blvd., Apt. 5
Circleville, CT 00345

Emsan@hayoo.com

(203) 555-2003
Fax: (203) 555-1924

Profile

Skilled research engineer with doctorate in materials engineering. Strong background in manufacturing process development and product improvement programs. Experienced in managing projects from conception to completion.

Education

Doctorate of Philosophy, University of Connecticut (2001)
Dissertation topic: Alloy modifications to Deotel 61 to reduce additions of strategic elements while retaining the original material properties

Master of Science, Massachusetts Institute of Technology (1999)
Theses topic: Optimizing the structure and properties of advanced cast irons to improve thermal fatigue resistance

Bachelor of Science, New York University (1997)

Publications

Doctoral Dissertation
Sanchez, *Metallurgy and Properties Research,* Pressman Publishers, 2002

Master's Thesis
Sanchez, *National Foundryman's Journal,* Wolcott & Associates, 2000

Invited Paper/Presentation
"Improved Product Performance Through Application of High-Strength Steels, Advanced Aluminum Alloys, Metal and Polymer Composites and Ceramics," 2002 International Tool Manufacturing Show, New York City, NY

Experience

1999-present

Research Engineer, Warren Industries, Stamford, CT
Manage projects for several externally sponsored and company-funded manufacturing development programs.
- Handle the entire spectrum of the traditional material removal processes, nonconventional techniques, tool design, process design and expert systems.
- Manage projects from conception through development planning, budgeting and scheduling; supervise technicians; present program highlights at executive conferences and trade shows.
- Revised research process to better coordinate with product marketing, resulting in more successful marketing programs and increased sales.

1999-2001

Professor's Assistant, Massachusetts Institute of Technology
Assisted and instructed undergraduate students in classroom and laboratory settings.
- Created all lecture and semester and final exam materials.
- Helped revise curriculum and graduation requirements for materials engineering students to better prepare them for the job market.

JAMES L. BENDER
701 Morningside Dr.
Woodland, MI 49003
(313) 555-2339
JBender@mymail.net

SKILLS PROFILE

- Manager with extensive background in quality control.
- Skilled in counseling customers on quality issues, establishing quality standards and solving quality-related problems.
- Experienced in meeting audit and survey requirements of current and prospective customers and in auditing suppliers to ensure conformity to customer specifications.
- Skilled in writing and maintaining quality manuals and in writing work instructions, quality procedures, in-process and final inspection forms.

WORK EXPERIENCE

1998-present

Quality Manager, Ridgeway Engineering, Detroit, MI
Manage internal quality of manufacturing records, certifications and requirements of individual customers. Supervise three inspectors.

- Handle internal and supplier audits, gauge calibration and implementation of SPC.
- Raised quality rating with major customer from 60% to 100% in two years and have had no rejections in three years.
- Earned Certified Supplier status with major customer and achieved no-inspection status for goods shipped from production plant to customer plant.
- Recommended and implemented new process, which increased production by 25% without jeopardizing quality.

1994-1998

Inspection Supervisor, Tube Forming, Corp., Woodland, MI

- Inspected in-process, welding, flouropenetrant, and final assembly.
- Handled fabrication, layout of aircraft engine tubing, and components for G.E., Allison, and Pratt & Whitney.
- Implemented new inspection process, which identified and led to correction of potential defects.

WORK EXPERIENCE

1992-1994   **Production Supervisor, Transmission Suppliers, Inc., Woodland, MI**
Supervised manufacturing and grinding of friction wafers for bonding to clutch and transmission pans. Met tolerances of ±00l.
▶ Used standard micrometers along with electronic mikes capable of averaging and SPC.
▶ Recommended new process, resulting in fewer casting cracks, higher product quality and $2 million in new business.
▶ Established new production procedure, which increased units produced by 40%.
▶ Wrote new quality manual, which established product specifications and standards necessary to meet customer requirements.

1990-1992   **Purchasing Agent/Shop Supervisor, Ridenour Systems, Detroit, MI**
Ordered and received materials. Controlled inventory. Supervised shop crew of six.
▶ Recommended new purchasing system, which eliminated delays, reduced paperwork and enhanced inventory control.
▶ Established standardized shop procedures, which resulted in more efficient operations and reduced training time.

1987-1990   **Machinist, National Filters, Detroit, MI**
Set up and operated engine and turret lathes, radial drills, milling machines and bullards. Inspected with tolerances of ±001. Served as group leader.
▶ Initiated new shop safety procedure, which reduced on-the-job injuries by 45%.

EDUCATION   Technical Vocational College, Woodland, MI (1992)
▶ Mechanical Drafting
▶ Machine Shop Supervision

National Filters, Detroit, MI (1988)
▶ Machine Shop
▶ Drafting

Michigan State University (1986-1987)
▶ General Studies

Martin S. Feeney
530 Winding Way
Gray Lake, MN 55735
(612) 555-2003
Martin@powermail.com

Objective

A full-time position as a music teacher at the elementary level

Summary of Skills
- Teaching license with endorsement in musical instruction.
- Experience tutoring elementary-aged children.
- Solid background as accompanist and assistant choral director.
- Skilled in designing hands-on learning centers.
- Ability to maintain discipline in the classroom while allowing children the freedom to discover the world of music.

Instructional Experience

Private Piano Instructor, Gray Lake, MN (1997 - present)
- Instruct 10 students in piano and the basics of learning and performing music.
- Host annual recital for students.
- Wrote and published instructional manual for beginning piano students.

Student Teacher, Gray Lake Elementary School and Warren Memorial Elementary School, Gray Lake School District, Gray Lake, MN (2002)
- Created daily lesson plans incorporating a variety of choral and instrumental music experiences for kindergarten through 5th-grade students in two schools.
- Worked with lead teacher to design a modified program for physically challenged students.
- Established program where students visit local nursing home to meet residents and teach them songs.
- Created learning centers combining experiences in music and math.

Tutor, Minnesota State University, East Ridge, MN (1994 -1996)
- Provided elementary-aged children with one-on-one education in math and reading.
- Worked with teachers to streamline two children from remedial to regular reading classes.

Musical Experience

Accompanist, Children's Choir, St. Luke's Methodist Church, Gray Lake, MN (1998 - present)
- Provide piano accompaniment for 20-member choir.
- Initiated instruction in rhythm instruments, which children now use to accompany their musical presentations

Assistant Choral Director, Chancel Choir, St. Luke's Methodist Church, Gray Lake, MN (1999 - present)
- Assist in selecting appropriate music for weekly worship services.
- Assist in directing choir during worship services.
- Initiated and direct combined handbell choir/chancel choir musical selections.

Orchestra member, Lakeview Community Theatre, Lakeview, MN (1997 - 1998)
- Provide keyboard accompaniment for two summer presentations.

Other Employment History

Account Analyst, Brownbury Financial Services, Minot, MN (2000 - present)
- Analyze and adjust accounts, including applying deferments and forbearances.
- Manually figure borrower and government interest for approximately 65 accounts per day.
- Served on team that recommended computer system upgrade, which enhanced system operation and reduced "bugs" and system "hang-ups."

Customer Service Representative, First National Bank, Minot, MN (1998 - 2000)
- Discussed available products, investigated account inquiries and answered customer service questions for approximately 100 customers daily.
- Assisted in training new service representatives.
- Revised filing system to accommodate centralization of customer service operations and provide easy filing/access for all new incoming correspondence.

Teller, First National Bank, Lakeview, MN (1996 - 1998)
- Accepted deposits, cashed checks and balanced teller window.
- Helped balance and maintain branch's daily records.
- Trained all part-time tellers.
- Recommended new verification process, which reduced customer account adjustment activity.

Education/Licensing

B.S. in Education, Otterbein University, Hudson, MN (2002)
  Endorsement in Musical Instruction
State of Minnesota Teachers License (2002)
B.S. in Liberal Arts, Minnesota State University, East Ridge, MN (1996)

MELINDA PRICE
505 E. Main St.
Shelbyville, TN 37160
(916) 555-2994

CAREER OBJECTIVE
Home designer for a major residential builder/developer

SKILLS PROFILE
- Well-developed drafting and technical skills
- Experience coordinating and managing subcontractors
- Knowledge of—and experience in—rezoning and meeting code specifications
- Excellent problem-solving skills
- Solid business and management background

EDUCATION
Associate's Degree in Architectural Technology, Tennessee University School of Science and Technology (2001)

ASSOCIATIONS / AWARDS
American Association of Architectural Engineers (2001 - present)
Honorable Mention, Best New Home Designer, Tennessee Architectural Society (2001)

EMPLOYMENT HISTORY
Home Designer, Browning Residence, Inc., Shelbyville, TN (2001 - present, part-time)
- Perform drafting and technical work for residential and commercial projects.
- Recommended and established new subcontracting procedure, which has reduced construction delays.
- Handle all rezoning and code specifications in commercial projects.

Branch Manager, First National Bank, Knoxville, TN (1995 - present)
- Supervised branch operations, new account personnel and the investment department.
- Guided branch through successful conversion to new computer system, products and procedures, resulting in fewer teller errors, faster posting and more efficient operations.

Senior Teller, First National Bank, Knoxville, TN (1992 - 1995)
- Assisted branch manager with all banking operations.
- Completed all teller work, including ensuring other tellers complied with proper procedures and adhered to policy changes.
- Established new computerized consumer loan process with main branch, which reduced paperwork and approval time.

Teller, First National Bank, Knoxville, TN (1990 - 1992)
- Provided customer service and new accounts service.
- Served as back-up to loan and investment departments.

LISA MAYS

80 West 106th St.   (502) 555-3945
Templeton, KY 42351   Fax: (502) 555-2996

CAREER OBJECTIVE

Agent with a regional real estate firm

SUMMARY OF QUALIFICATIONS

Communication/Marketing Skills
- Designed customer information guide for first-time home buyers, which enhances bank's image as knowledgeable lender.
- Nearly 70% of customers who visit bank and take brochure return for mortgage loan, although bank not always offering lowest lending rates.
- Addressed market demand by developing automated withdrawal procedure for payments on bank-held mortgages.
- Handled retail sales for floral designer and introduced new gift line that increased sales 25%.

Leadership Skills
- Served on team that tripled mortgage turnover for bank.
- Recommended, adapted and entered loan processing functions into computer system, resulting in faster approval time.
- Recommended new computer software that improved posting time and decreased errors.

Financial Skills
- Thorough knowledge of mortgage loans, points and interest, and how they affect the buyer.
- Process mortgage loans, including FHA and VA loans.

EMPLOYMENT

Mortgage Loan Processor, First National Bank, Templeton, KY (1999-present)

Bookkeeper, First National Bank, Templeton, KY (1996-1999)

Floral Designer/Sales Clerk, Whitmer's Flowers and Gifts, Nora, KY (1994-1996)

EDUCATION/LICENSING

2002	Real Estate License, State of Kentucky
2001, 1998	Division of Continuing Studies, Cutter University, Akron, KY Courses in real estate law (2001) and data processing (1998)
2000	National Banking Institute, Frankfort, KY Courses in FHA and VA loan processing
1994	A.S. Degree in Horticulture, Cutter University, Akron, KY

WILLIAM J. BENNETT
725 Otter Lane
Wausau, WI 54554

(715) 555-6006   BillJB@mycomp.net   Fax: (715) 555-2245

SUMMARY

Skilled executive with extensive background in—and thorough knowledge of—bank operations and mortgage, commercial and consumer lending. Experienced in developing and implementing competitive programs and services. Exceptional organizational, analytical and managerial skills.

EXPERIENCE
1986-present

First City Bank, Wausau, WI
Vice President, 1998-present
- Supervise 60 employees and total bank operations for main office and three branches with a total of $50 million in assets.
- Developed and continue to implement new business development plan, which includes calling on customers and prospects while enhancing bank's image in the community.
- Established new IRA procedures and Discount Brokerage Service, which expanded customer service offerings and created new business.

Manager, 1994-1998
- Performed branch employee evaluations, scheduled continued education and training and assisted with career and sales development.
- Managed all daily branch operations, including opening and closing of branch, implementing and maintaining policies and procedures, ensuring compliance with federal banking regulations, customer contact and conflict resolution, and overdraft authorization.
- Developed and implemented bank's enhanced automated teller machine system, which provided a new, high-tech, competitive service.

Loan Officer, 1991-1994
- Developed, originated, documented, and closed commercial, consumer, and mortgage loans, concentrating in residential construction lending and commercial lending.
- Expanded business development to include deposits and loans, which increased loan business 25%.
- Developed and implemented indirect lending program, which filled a need as identified by customer feedback.

Assistant Branch Manager, 1986-1991
- Handled most daily branch operations and trained all new employees.
- Supervised successful conversion from manual to computerized record-keeping, resulting in enhanced customer service and account reporting.
- Coordinated construction and on-schedule completion of new branch.

EDUCATION

B.S. in Business Management, University of Wisconsin, Beloit 1986

MEGHAN S. WILGUS

505 W. Delaware
Hagerstown, MD 21741

(301) 555-1221
MSWilgus@mailbox.net

PROFILE

More than 10 years experience in production supervision, with special emphasis on scheduling. Skilled in personnel supervision, training, and vendor relations. Adept at revising current processes to improve plant operations.

WORK HISTORY
1989-present

Waverly Industries, Hagerstown, MD
Production Control Supervisor, 1996-present
Supervise and train up to eight production schedulers in machine shop, polishing, and assembly departments. Create daily and weekly device schedules based on monthly master schedule output.
- Initiated duty to serve as material dispatcher and outside vendor contact, which provides link between operations and has resulted in improved vendor relations and long-term contracts from three major vendors.
- Designed new assembly process for product, which reduced assembly time 30% and increased production 50%, without jeopardizing quality.

Production Scheduler-Assembly, 1993-1996
Created daily device dispatch list and procured material from shop floor and warehouse for dispatch list.
- Worked with machine shop, polishing, and plating departments to revise procedures, resulting in smooth material flow through manufacturing plant.

Master Production Scheduler, 1991-1993
Created and maintained master production schedule for all "push pad" devices on monthly basis, using backlog, forecasts and historical data.
- Devised daily update system for master schedule, which provided additional scheduling information by logging return of completed dispatch list from shop floor.
- Initiated evaluation of item master maintenance and system de-bugging, which resulted in error-free, standardized coding system.

Project Engineer, 1989-1991
Created and maintained product data management concerning all shop routings, time studies, tooling, and other information.
- Brought several vendor operations in-house, resulting in annual savings of $200,000.

EDUCATION

B.S. in Industrial Management, University of Maryland, College Park, 1989

ACTIVITIES

Secretary, Maryland Businesswomen's Association, Hagerstown Chapter
Board Member, Boys' and Girls' Club of Hagerstown

SUSAN J. SMOCK

24 Countryside Lane   (702) 555-9776
Jackson, NV 89934   Smock4@alo.com

OBJECTIVE   A position as a sales representative or account manager with a major
                       dental products supplier.

SUMMARY OF SKILLS

- Extensive training and experience in expanded dental assistant duties.
- Thorough knowledge of dental hygiene products and their use in proper oral hygiene and soft tissue management.
- Experienced in encouraging and "selling" quality, preventive dentistry to patients.
- Strong and successful background in retail sales, purchasing and management.
- Skilled in organizing and presenting product seminars.

DENTAL EXPERIENCE

1999-present   Expanded Duties Dental Assistant, Dr. Eric L. Hussong, DDS, Jackson, NV

1996-1999   Expanded Duties Dental Assistant, Dr. Brenda S. Walker, DDS, Silverton, NV

SALES EXPERIENCE

1996-present   **Sales Clerk,** Sarah's Boutique, Jackson, NV
- Handle floor sales and assist and advise customers in selecting purchases.
- Design innovative window displays, which increase customer traffic in store.
- Recommended and implemented introduction of new sportswear line, which increased sales 25%.
- Created sales promotion, which increased ready-to-wear sales 35%.

1992-1995   **Sales Manager,** The Silver Box, Silverton, NV
- Completed sales and purchasing duties for women's clothing store.
- Created and implemented new, upscale "look" for store, including new floor plan, display ideas and logo.
- Introduced new shopping service using customer profile program, which allowed for gift purchases by telephone and increased sales 15%.
- Consistently exceeded sales objectives by at least 30%.
- Assumed additional responsibility and assisted in business expansion by managing all purchases for new store in nearby community.

CERTIFICATION

1995   Expanded Duties Certification, Nevada University School of Dentistry, Carson City

Teresa Seguso

501 Hampton Dr. • Lakeview, KY • 40990 • (502) 555-9223 • Fax: (502) 555-1074

Objective

A position as human resources manager of a company with 1,200-plus employees

Summary of Qualifications

Excellent human resources background, including applicant screening; employee orientation, evaluation and placement; safety and training; and benefits planning. Experienced in developing and implementing new safety, training and employee orientation programs.

Work Experience

Human Resources Assistant, Allied Associates, Lakeview, KY, 2001-present

- Designed new employee orientation package and established and facilitated all new employee activities and sessions, which provides (for the first time) continuity in all company and benefit information presented verbally and in writing.
- Assist vice president in budget reconciliation and other forecasting/planning activities.
- Assisted in administering a revised employee evaluation program, which allows for improvement on identified problem areas before final evaluation.
- Prepare confidential material for grievance and other personnel-related meetings.
- Researched and currently implementing flex benefits program, which allows employees to design their own benefits packages, resulting in higher employee satisfaction.

Training and Safety Assistant, McMurtry and Co., Lexington, KY, 1999-2001

- Worked with training manager to develop new, in-house computer software training courses, saving $3,500 annually in outside training costs.
- Assisted training manager in developing Secretarial Training Program, which has successfully standardized procedures and enhanced office work flow.
- Revised safety manual and initiated OSHA update bulletins, which reduced on-the-job injuries by 55% and reduced OSHA non-compliance warnings by 75%.
- Assisted in evaluating and scheduling all outside executive training programs.

Personnel Assistant, McMurtry and Co., Lexington, KY, 1997-1999

- Administered temporary service personnel program, which involved 40% of the secretarial and hourly work force on site.
- Scheduled and screened full-time job applicants and coordinated applicant testing and pre-employment physicals.
- Established and administered service award program.
- Created job descriptions for hourly employees.

Education

B.S. in Business Administration, University of Kentucky, Lexington (1997)

MONICA GREEN

37 Bayberry Court
Gateway, GA 30372
(404) 555-4299

SKILLS PROFILE

- Well-rounded background in human resources, training, safety, operations, and consumer affairs.
- Excellent experience developing and implementing a variety of corporate programs, including those that must comply with corporate, state, and federal agency guidelines.
- Skilled in developing department budgets and creating department objectives.
- Experienced in writing and delivering presentations for executive meetings.

WORK HISTORY

2000-present

Sr. Administrative Assistant, Operations & Safety, Ralston Corp., Atlanta, GA
- Develop yearly budgetary forecasts for three departments and ensure forecasts meet corporate guidelines.
- Served on team that created short- and long-term department objectives in accordance with company goals.
- Administer safety program at local plant and work with safety coordinators at company's three other plants to address safety issues presented by employees.
- Updated and implemented safety training program for product manufacturing groups at all plants, which reduced on-the-job injuries by 75%.
- Maintain OSHA log, analyze incidents at local site and review proposed regulations for impact on local plant.

1995-2000

Consumer Affairs Specialist, Ralston Corp., Atlanta, GA
- Initiated new tracking system to follow up consumer letters sent to other departments for response; response time to consumer increased by 50%.
- Achieved top ranking among eight other team members for toll-free number performance (efficiency and effectiveness in handling consumer calls).
- Prepared quarterly reports, graphs and quality assurance grids for two products.
- Developed Degradability Response Letter and drafted microwave, degradability, and recycling information for product packages.

WORK HISTORY (Continued)

1994-1995

Secretary/Personnel Assistant, Human Resources, Ralston Corp., Atlanta, GA
- Worked with training manager to develop and implement New Employee Orientation Program (NEOP).
- Wrote New Employee Reference Guide, which helped employees better understand the company, its operations, and who to contact with questions.
- Assisted training manager in developing Secretarial Training Program, resulting in a more efficient, productive staff.
- Assisted vice president in budget reconciliation and other activities.

1993-1994

Human Resources Clerk, Goodman and Sons, Inc., Waverly, GA
- Scheduled full-time job applicants and coordinated applicant testing and pre-employment physicals.
- Created and implemented service award program, including determining and ordering awards for years of service and supplying information to company newsletter.
- Assisted in introducing flex benefits program and facilitated employee meetings, which helped gain employee acceptance.

1991-1993

Confidential Temporary, McClure Temporary Services, Atlanta, GA
- Worked primarily in personnel departments of larger companies, handling information related to full-time job applicants.
- Created, updated and verified clerical job descriptions with appropriate department heads.

EDUCATION

2000-present Undergraduate studies in Business Administration, Beacom College, Atlanta, GA

1989-1991 Undergraduate studies in Personnel Management, Beacom College, Atlanta, GA

ACTIVITIES/ MEMBERSHIPS

- Treasurer, Ralston Activities Committee
- Member, Society of Consumer Affairs Professionals
- Member, National Association of Personnel Women

STEVEN T. HAWKINS
602 Brandenway Court
Williams, CA 95510
www.Hawkinshome.com

(707) 555-8324   Fax: (707) 555-1797

Objective: To apply my small business and international experience to a corporate management position.

Profile: Self-employed construction project manager with extensive supervisory and carpentry background. Successfully operated own businesses for 15 years, including completing and winning major bids, managing a labor force and finishing projects on schedule and on budget. Experienced at supervising and completing projects in other countries. Fluent in Spanish.

Work Experience:

1991 - present **Hawkins Enterprises, Williams, CA**
Owner/Manager
Complete interior finish projects, including submitting bids, supervising operations, hiring and training labor, purchasing materials and handling payroll and customer relations.
- Trained local labor force, supervised product shipment, and successfully managed projects in France, Hong Kong, and Ecuador, completing all projects on time and on budget.
- Successfully bid for and completed various interior projects for financial institutions and small and large businesses in two-state area.
- Completed eight spec houses in the $800,000 range.
- Completed a variety of general construction projects involving residential remodeling and agricultural facilities.

1988 - 1991 **Movable Walls, Rosewood, CA**
Owner/Manager
Completed interior finish projects for national company dealing in movable wall partitions.
- Established installation capabilities for national dealer in three-state area, resulting in 40% sales increase for dealer and 46 new major business opportunities.
- Completed 32 projects for small and large businesses.
- Hired and trained own labor force.

1984 - 1988 **Interiors, Inc., Rosewood, CA**
Area Manager
Expanded market for movable wall partitions throughout northern California.
- Consulted with prospective clients and provided cost, benefits, and installation schedule information, creating new markets and increasing sales 35%.
- Managed a six-person field staff and two-person office staff.
- Personally supervised 26 projects.

Work Experience:

1984 - 1988 **The Design Company, Rosewood, CA**
Installation Training Manager
Supervised training program for company installers and supervisors.
- Developed and implemented new training manual and training program, resulting in more efficient, productive installers, higher customer satisfaction, and fewer design errors.
- Served as member of product development team, which created 10 standard, easy-to-install office designs to meet small-office market demands.

1981 - 1984 **Hickman Co., Greenville, CA**
Carpenter Foreman
Managed construction projects in northern California and western Nevada.
- Successfully completed 25 major projects on time.
- Supervised union carpenters.
- Secured seven new construction projects for the company.

1981 - 1982 **Skilled Carpenter (self-employed), Wooster, CA**
- Completed general construction and specialty trim work.
- Recommended new trim technique, which reduced finishing time and material costs and increased durability.
- Remodeled own Victorian home to original design and appearance.

Education: Associate's Degree in Supervision, University of Northern California (1984)
Associate's Degree in Business Management, State Community College (1989)

Memberships: West Coast Carpenter's Association, area representative (1992 - 1995)

MARGARET K. COOPER

1815 W. Barner St.
Anchorage, AK 99506

(907) 555-6887
MKCooper@mailstar.net

SKILLS SUMMARY Supervisor with seven years accounting experience in medical billing, collections, and patient payment plans. Solid background in computer software, computer operations, and training. Consistently recruited to trouble-shoot and establish billing/collection policies and procedures.

PROFESSIONAL EXPERIENCE

March 2001 - present   **Patient Accounts Manager, Chugach Orthopedics, P.C., Anchorage, AK**
Supervise three employees in billing office for four orthopedic surgeons. Arrange financial payment plans with patients and set up in-house collection policies.
- Recruited to reorganize billing office and establish new job responsibilities to improve work flow and create opportunities for cross-training and career development.
- Apprise front and back office staff on all current insurance policies and requirements.
- Renew physicians' credentials with contracted PPOs, HMOs and other networks.
- Established new collection and patient payment policies, which have reduced uncollected bills by 35%.

April 2000 - March 2001   **Account Analyst, Union Hospital Physician Billing Office, Anchorage, AK**
Maintained two deposit reports. Managed money for 14 physicians, including all current over-the-counter collections.
- Assumed temporary position to assist in training 30 employees in registration and scheduling on new computer software system.
- Hired, trained, and supervised temporary employees on old computer system.
- Supervised temporary employees for collection of old accounts receivable.

June 1999 - April 2000   **Business Office Manager, Anchorage General Hospital, Anchorage, AK**
Supervised nine employees, including front office, billing, collections, payroll and admissions personnel.
- Hired to revise procedures for collecting patient and insurance portions of patient accounts; reduced turnaround from nine weeks to two.
- Handled all daily deposits, audited general ledger, and prepared month-end reports.
- Conducted financial interviews with patients still in-house.

PROFESSIONAL EXPERIENCE

May 1998 - June 1999

Accounts Receivable Manager, Bayside Medical Group, Fairbanks, AK
Supervised six employees in billing office for 14 physicians. Managed office's computer operation, including training staff on accounting software.
- Recruited to establish and manage billing and collections for satellite Occupational Health office, posting 98% collection rate.
- Processed refunds and prepared all accounts receivable reports.

May 1997 - May 1998

Accounting Assistant, Yukon Hospital, Fairbanks, AK
Handled data processing, including computer input of cash, charges, adjustments, daily census, and admissions.
- Assumed temporary position to supervise all data input for new software program.

June 1996 - May 1997

Accounts Payable Clerk, Hobson Living Centers, Seattle, WA
Edited and batched invoices from 15 nursing homes.
- Conducted training seminars for 15 out-of-state nursing homes.

June 1995 - June 1996

Internal Audit Clerk, Hobson Living Centers, Seattle, WA
Audited patients' personal funds and audited payables to general ledger. Served as secretary to field analyst.
- Promoted after one year.

EDUCATION

Associate's Degree in Accounting,
Lincoln Community College, WA (1994)

ACTIVITIES

Volunteer, English Estates Nursing Home, Anchorage
Math Tutor, Gannett Elementary School, Anchorage

STEVEN R. RHOADES
401 Brightwood Dr.
Glen Ellyn, IL 60312
(708) 555-3565
Steve022@quick.net

CAREER GOAL

To secure a position with a U.S. Senator's or U.S. Representative's office

PROFILE

- Working knowledge of legislative committees, constituent relations, and the legislative process.
- Experienced in legislative research and in reporting findings necessary to support specific legislation.
- Excellent communication and problem-solving skills.
- Award-winning manager with five years experience in customer relations.

EDUCATION

Masters of Public Affairs, Northwestern University, Evanston, IL (expected 2003)

Bachelor of Science in Management, *Cum Laude*, University of Illinois, Urbana/Champaign (1998)

WORK EXPERIENCE

Illinois House of Representatives, Springfield
Legislative Internship, (2002-present)
Work closely on daily basis with state representatives. Handle daily written and verbal contact with constituents. Complete comprehensive research and special projects for representatives. Monitor various committee work and the general session.

- Served on team that researched legislation and conducted meetings with constituents for Senators Duvall and Hudnut regarding Governor Wilson's 2003 budget proposal.
- Presented ideas and research findings, which senators used in legislative session to support proposal, resulting in House approval of the bill.

WORK EXPERIENCE

Blackwell Entertainment Network, Chicago, IL
Sales Service Executive (2001-2002)
Handled national cable schedules on two cable networks. Maintained client and agency relations through written correspondence, phone contact and sales calls. Compiled all needed research. Prepared and presented research materials.

- Recommended and implemented new research tool, which provided more accurate information than current methods and led to increased sales.

Blackwell Entertainment Network, Chicago, IL
Sales Assistant (2000-2001)
Ordered and serviced client cable schedules. Maintained all inter-company sales/budget figures for Midwest/Chicago area.

- Consistently received high customer satisfaction ratings and was named Outstanding Sales Assistant for three consecutive months (January-March 2001).

Chicago Tribune, Chicago, IL
District Circulation Manager, Elmhurst (1999-2000)
Supervised daily circulation for approximately 12,000 customers. Managed carrier force of nearly 160 independent contractors. Insured proper payment of bills by independent contractors and consumers. Directly supervised two salaried service managers and three part-time district assistants.

- Developed new incentive program, which increased circulation by rewarding carriers for developing new customers.
- Named District Manager of the Month (February 2000).

Service Manager (1998-1999)
Managed more than 80 carriers serving 4,100 customers. Supervised bill collection, payment, and route management.

- Initiated and implemented new pick-up and loading process, which reduced carriers' waiting time by one hour on weekdays and by two hours on Sunday and resulted in more timely delivery.
- Promoted to District Circulation Manager after only nine months.

RELATED ACTIVITIES

Election Precinct Judge, Kendall County, IL (2000-2001)
Election Precinct Inspector, Kendall County, IL (2001-2002)
Member, Speaker's Bureau, Illinois Voter Registration Council (2002-present)

PAUL M. VOIGHT
1034 W. Merrick Dr.
Greencastle, IN 46909
(317) 555-8008

OBJECTIVE

A position in warehouse operations management with a large, interstate retailer or distributor.

SKILLS SUMMARY

Varied but accomplished background in operations, sales and customer service. Excel in operations management, especially warehouse traffic management and distribution. Experienced in contracting and scheduling freight operations. Skilled in reorganizing operations to save money.

EXPERIENCE

Operations Assistant, Replay Records, Indianapolis, IN, 2002-present
- Assist in managing and supervising central warehouse operations, including traffic management and distribution.
- Contract, coordinate and schedule freight operations between four stores.
- Recommended new handling procedure, which better protects fragile warehouse inventory.
- Assisted in reorganizing warehouse operations and freight distribution, resulting in $75,000 savings annually.

Sales Associate, Lewis Jewelers, Greencastle, IN, 2001-2002
- Handled floor sales and assisted customers with purchases.
- Designed and implemented new gift registry, which provided computer print out of customer's gift list.
- Assisted in daily bookkeeping and monthly statements.
- Developed special wedding sales promotion, which expanded wedding registries by 35%.

Insurance Underwriter, American Insurance Co., Indianapolis, IN, 2000-2001
- Analyzed individual risks for potential liability and property losses.
- Communicated verbally and in writing with agents.

Customer Service Representative, First City Bank, Greencastle, IN, 1999-2000
- Completed daily business transactions, including teller and safe-deposit duties.
- Assisted in balancing branch's daily books.
- Opened new accounts and closed existing accounts.
- Recommended new safe-deposit procedure, which reduced paperwork.

EDUCATION

DePauw University, Greencastle, IN (1998-1999)
- 21 credit hours in general studies

Mark T. Turner • 233 W. Allen Dr. • Wellington, Pa. • 19032 • (215) 555-8828 • MTT@mail.net

Summary of Qualifications

Award-winning national sales manager with proven sales and organizational skills. Ability to train and maintain an enthusiastic, productive staff. Excellent experience in account management, reducing projected store losses and exceeding all sales goals.

Work Experience

National Rentals, Inc. (1997 - present)

Manage sales, rental contracts, repossessions, inventory, and computerized payroll and bookkeeping. Arrange store displays, handle local marketing and advertising. Train and evaluate up to 10 employees.

Store Manager, Wellington, Pa.

(2001 - present)
- Increased revenues and rental units 25%.
- Named to Star Performers Club, Eastern Division.
- Winner of special incentive contest for unit gain, Eastern Division.
- Named Sales Store of the Month, Eastern Division (October 2001).

Store Manager, Brookville, Ind.

(1999 - 2001)
- Named National Store Manager of the Year for fiscal 2000.
- Achieved top 1% of sales nationwide.
- Increased revenues and rental units 55%.
- Named Sales Store of the Month, Market 121 (June 2000).
- Reduced projected store losses by 40%.

Store Manager, Wayfare, Ohio

(1998 - 1999)
- First account manager to advance to store manager in less than one year.
- Named Sales Store of the Month, all divisions (June and July 1998).
- Achieved fourth place in unit gain for new stores, all divisions (July 1998).
- Earned fourth in store performance income for new stores, all divisions (June 1998).
- Placed second in exceeding plan on average price of rental agreements for new stores, all divisions (June 1998).

Account Manager, Berlington, Mich.

(1997 - 1998)
- Initiated new contract review program, which reduced repossessions 25%.
- Eliminated account backlog and computerized all records.

Education

B.S. in Marketing, Southern Michigan University, Sturgis, May 1997

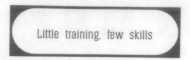

ANNA GILROY
323 South Avon Drive
Milton, NY 10945
(914) 555-2909
AnnaGilroy@access.net

OBJECTIVE
A position as general office clerk for a major corporation.

SKILLS PROFILE
- Ability to operate Lilly 5000 copy/collating machine.
- Knowledge and experience with corporate mailroom procedures.
- Good filing and organizational skills.
- Experience in handling confidential paperwork.
- Ability to take accurate phone messages and deliver messages promptly.
- Good customer relations background.

EMPLOYMENT HISTORY
Copy machine attendant, Hodges, Wilson and Pickard, Milton, NY (2000-present)
- Copy and collate all projects (including confidential papers) for 25-lawyer firm.
- Successfully complete all jobs by time requested.
- Coordinate delivery of large projects with mailroom clerk.
- Initiated "rush procedure," which guarantees "rush" copy projects of 1,000 total pages or less will be completed within 30 minutes of submission.
- Enhanced copy room operations.
- Won the quarterly "Employee Suggestion Award" for "rush procedure".

Mailroom clerk, Hodges, Wilson and Pickard, Milton, NY (1996-2000)
- Accurately filed and delivered mail to all company departments.
- Suggested new mail code system, which reduced filing errors and increased timely delivery.
- Computed amount of postage required for outgoing mail, depending on weight and classification.
- Covered phones for word processing clerk during clerk's lunch break.

Waitress/Cashier, The Corner Restaurant, Harris, NY (1994-1996)
- Took orders, served restaurant patrons and assisted at the cash register.
- Created "Tuesday Casino Night" theme, including food and games, which doubled the number of customers on a typically slow night.

EDUCATION
River Valley High School, Harris, NY (Diploma, 1994)

GLENN T. ROBINSON
55 S. Bailey Ct.
Baton Rouge, LA 70332
(504) 555-6992

OBJECTIVE

Courier

SKILLS PROFILE

- Excellent driving, safety and attendance record.
- Thorough knowledge of area roads, highways and regional airport.
- Proven record of completing all deliveries on schedule.
- Experienced in operating heavy machinery.
- Good background in assembling products and printed materials.

EMPLOYMENT HISTORY

Courier, Miller Industries, Baton Rouge, LA (1999-2002)
- Only driver/courier to log 7,000 miles with no accidents or violations.
- Served as liaison and helped develop delivery schedule with new overnight service company located at airport.
- Initiated "orange cone" system, which reduced backing accidents in courier group and earned company safety award.

Equipment Operator, Street Department, City of Baton Rouge, LA (1997-1998)
- Worked on city street and bridge repair projects.
- Operated heavy machinery, including steam roller and backhoe.
- Served on team to evaluate new street cleaning machines; recommended model which reduced work crew time by five hours per week.

Assembler, Taylor Printing, Inc., Baton Rouge, LA (1995-1997)
- Collated and assembled printing projects.
- Operated machines that scored and folded brochures.

Assembler, Prairie Industries, Baton Rouge, LA (1994)
- Produced Christmas garland and trees.
- Provided general labor in assembly plant for seasonal products.

PHYLLIS KRAMER
55 Prairie Lane
Coatsville, ND 58365
(701) 555-3002

OBJECTIVE
A secondary position in biology, general science and/or physical science for grade levels 7 to 12.

SKILLS PROFILE
✦ Experienced in creating lesson plans, designing laboratory experiments and maintaining disciplined atmosphere.
✦ Knowledgeable in designing and evaluating computer science labs.
✦ Strong volunteer/instructional background.
✦ Mature and experienced in working with children of all ages.
✦ Excellent rapport with students.
✦ Skilled in successful fund raising, event planning and program development.

**EDUCATION/
ENDORSEMENTS**
2001-present   Graduate Studies, North Dakota State University
1991   B.S. in Biology, *with honors,* North Dakota State University
               ✦ Endorsements in General Sciences and Physical Sciences

STUDENT TEACHING
1990   **Student Teacher, Marshall High School, Marshall, ND**
       ✦ Taught first-year biology and chemistry.
       ✦ Assisted in second-year biology.
       ✦ Created all daily lessons, tests, laboratory experiments and semester tests for both biology and chemistry.

INSTRUCTIONAL EXPERIENCE
2001-present   **Substitute Teacher, Coatsville Jr./Sr. High School, Coatsville, ND**
       ✦ Instruct students in all subject areas.
       ✦ Complete lesson plans as directed and provide teacher with feedback.
       ✦ Maintain disciplined academic atmosphere.

1999-present   **Volunteer Science Instructor, Coatsville Community School Corp., Coatsville, ND**
       ✦ Assist, instruct, and provide feedback to junior- and senior-high school students on a variety of lab projects.
       ✦ Work with students on defining their research and hypotheses and determining their variables for successful science fair projects.

INSTRUCTIONAL
EXPERIENCE (cont.)

1996-1999   **Church School Teacher/Vacation Bible School Teacher, First United Presbyterian Church, Coatsville, ND**
+ Instructed elementary and preschool children each Sunday and during week-long summer Bible School sessions.
+ Created lesson plans and designed related activities.
+ Coordinated dramatic presentations for worship services.
+ Recommended program improvements, which resulted in self-contained learning units and increased church school attendance.

1991-1993   **Science Teacher, Prairie Senior High School, Bismarck, ND**
+ Taught first-year biology and second-year chemistry students.
+ Designed special laboratory experiments, which increased interaction and idea-sharing among students.
+ Coordinated annual science fair and guided students in their research and development of successful projects.
+ Led committee which designed a state-of-the-art classroom computer lab to provide hands-on learning experiences and better prepare students for higher education.

VOLUNTEER/ORGANIZATIONAL
EXPERIENCE

1999-current   **Member, Textbook Adoption Committee, Coatsville Community School System, Coatsville, ND**
+ Review elementary-level English, science and mathematics text books and recommend which should be included in curriculum.

2000-2001   **Officer, Coatsville Elementary Parent/Teacher Organization, Coatsville, ND**
+ Organized most successful fund-raising carnival to date.
+ Planned and implemented first-ever T-shirt sales program.
+ Created first-ever Christmas sales program.

1999-2000   **Officer, "Ministry of Care," First United Presbyterian Church, Coatsville, ND**
+ Created and implemented program to serve church's outreach needs.
+ Organized volunteers to call on hospital patients and visitors to church.
+ Developed program comprising eight committees and 200 volunteers.

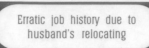
Erratic job history due to
husband's relocating

GRETCHEN MULHONEY

425 E. Kilroy Place ◆ Eastlake, Ohio ◆ 44110 ◆ (216) 555-9223 ◆ Gretch@alo.net

OBJECTIVE
A position as a business manager for a major retailer.

SKILLS/ABILITIES
Financial
- Skilled in handling credit reporting, collections, bookkeeping and installment contracts for retailer with $3 million in annual sales.
- Experienced in managing collections and developing payment plan programs, which have increased collections by 25%.
- Adept in handling all monthly payments on personal accounts for business owner and balancing all accounts monthly.

Management/Organizational
- Skilled in office management, including accounts payable, accounts receivable, daily and monthly postings, financial statements, monthly and quarterly taxes, and payroll for business generating $5 million annually in sales.
- Experienced in managing rental income properties, including collecting rent, depositing and posting income for 60 properties, and paying expenses through eight different accounts.
- Able to train new employees and inform current employees of new policies and procedures and ensure compliance.
- Skilled in developing successful business office procedures, resulting in productive office operations, accurate records, and a well-functioning staff.

Communication/Customer Service
- Skilled in providing information and counseling bank customers on account services that would best serve their needs.
- Experienced in initiating special services for car repair customers, resulting in increased customer satisfaction and increased return business.

WORK EXPERIENCE
Business Manager, Anderson Buick, Eastlake, Ohio (2000-present)
Business Manager, Kessler Chevrolet, Flint, Mich. (1997-2000)
Office Manager, Meyers Furniture, Merrillville, Ind. (1993-1997)
Savings Department Supervisor, Union National Bank, Lansing, Ill. (1990-1993)
Teller, Wisconsin State Bank, Whitewater, Wis. (1987-1990)

EDUCATION
Associate's Degree in Supervision, Illinois University (1993)
Financial Courses, American Institute of Banking (1990-1992)

HONORS
Business Managers Award from district office (1998, 1999, 2001, 2002)

ANNE K. JOHNSON

501 Brenden Way • Twinsburg, IN • 46269 • (219) 555-1924 • AKJohnson@alo.net

OBJECTIVE

A position as a fund raiser/volunteer organizer for a nonprofit organization.

SKILLS/ABILITIES

Management/Organization

- Coordinated philanthropic organization's "Tour of Homes" fund raiser for three years, raising $3,600 the first year, $4,200 the second year, and $5,300 the third year.
- Served two terms as president of philanthropic group; increased membership 30%; established new fund raiser that brought in $1,500 annually to benefit the community.
- Recruited and organized, for four years, up to 40 volunteers for church's annual summer vacation Bible school.
- Served as secretary for school Parent/Teacher Organization for two years.
- Chaired and organized PTO school carnival which raised $2,500 and was the most successful fund-raising event in 10 years.
- Assisted in coordinating volunteer drivers for senior services organization. Teaching/ training
- Planned curriculum for vacation Bible school for two years.
- Planned curriculum and taught preschool and kindergarten Sunday School classes for three years.
- Tutored (through library program) four 1st- and 2nd-grade students in reading.
- Hosted story hour with children's librarian at local public library, including scheduling special guests and organizing visits to the police and fire departments, post office, and more.

Communication/Leadership

- Developed and distributed brochures for local public library about children's programs, which nearly doubled attendance at the programs.
- Helped create brochure explaining local, state, and federal services and funds for food and child care assistance for low-income families.
- Served on team with representatives from county agencies to develop and implement child care provider training and certification program to improve the quality of child care offered in private homes.

VOLUNTEER WORK HISTORY

Twinsburg Public Library, Children's Department, Tutoring Department, (1999-pesent)
Twinsburg Christian Church, Children's Education Department, (1998-present)
Twinsburg Public Schools, Parent/Teacher Organization, (2001-present)
Psi Iota Xi national philanthropic sorority, Omega Chapter, (1994-present)
Greensboro County Senior Services, Volunteer Transportation (2000-present)
Greensboro County Youth Action Coalition, Child Care Services Team, (2001-present)

EDUCATION

Bachelor of Arts in Consumer and Family Sciences, Indiana State University, Terre Haute (1992)

MICHELLE R. HAUGHTON

33 Lakeview Dr.
Hunter Lake, MN 56453
MichelleRH@hayoo.com

218·555·2993

Cell: 218·555·9901

OBJECTIVE   A supervisory position in project management.

PROFILE
- Six years engineering, design, processing, and development experience in the automotive industry.
- Skilled in working with team to design and develop innovative advance engine products.
- Holder of two patents.

SKILLS/ABILITIES

Design
- Served on team that designed and developed innovative automotive engine project from concept layout through vehicle testing on three engine phases.
- Experienced with finite element, thermodynamic modeling, design verification, failure mode effects analysis, design for manufacture and assembly.
- Able to incorporate combustion knowledge into base engine design.

Development
- Developed bench and dynamometer test plans for engines and components.
- Use rapid prototype techniques to save material budget and time.
- Apply statistical techniques to develop and design experiments.

Process
- Designed parts for all major casting techniques in ferrous and non-ferrous alloys.
- Experienced with high- and low-volume machining processes, including geometric tolerances.

EMPLOYMENT HISTORY

Glasgow Motor Corporation, St. Paul, MN
- Product Engineer (1998-present)
- Cooperative Education Student, Product Development (1996-1998)

EDUCATION

Master of Science in Mechanical Engineering, University of Minnesota (expected 2004)
Bachelor of Science in Mechanical Engineering, University of Minnesota (1999)

NANCY GILSON

4665 S 250 W ◆ North Platte, IN ◆ 41004 ◆ (219) 555-9293

CAREER GOAL

A position as a food services manager or catering supervisor.

SUMMARY OF EXPERIENCE

Organizational/management skills

- Organize, host, plan menu, and supervise preparation of all food for 500 guests at annual Indiana Cattle Association picnic (23 years).
- Plan and organize annual State Fair picnic for more than 400 cattle owners and guests, including securing sponsorships and donations of soft drinks, paper, and plastic goods (12 years).
- Organize up to 120 volunteers and supervise food preparation and forecasting for State Fair beef tent, which brings in $100,000 annually for the state cattle association (10 years).
- Organize and supervise up to 25 volunteers for church's annual fall craft fair/luncheon; have successfully planned and met budget for 11 years and raised more than $7,000 for church and charitable causes.
- Planned, purchased goods, organized up to 10 volunteers, and helped prepare nutritious snacks for weekly church school classes (7 years).
- Chair meal portion of home economic club's annual fall bazaar and luncheon, including purchasing goods and supervising food preparation; for 8 years have consistently brought food purchases in under budget and exceeded fund-raising goals by 20%.

Financial/budgeting skills

- Skilled in handling computerized bookkeeping for 1,200-acre grain and 250-head cattle farming operation.
- Initiated and completed data entry from manual to computerized record-keeping system, resulting in improved account analysis, improved report generation for loan/banking and tax purposes, and reduced bookkeeping time.
- Experienced in monthly farm and household budgeting and timely payment of personal and business accounts.

Other related skills

- Experienced in planning and creating low-fat, low-sugar, and low-sodium meals.
- Skilled in presenting knowledgeable instruction on proper food handling and storage.

EDUCATION

Bachelor of Science in Home Economics, Purdue University, West Lafayette, Ind.

MEMBERSHIPS

President, Secretary, Treasurer, Out and About Home Ec Club, Warren County, Ind.
President, Treasurer, Advisory Board, United Methodist Church, North Platte, Ind.

Marcia T. Gestault
105 S. Esplanade Dr.
Greenville, MI. 49002
(313) 555-3203

CAREER OBJECTIVE   To secure a position in collegiate student affairs, involving program development, advisory, and/or communication responsibilities.

SUMMARY OF QUALIFICATIONS

Program development skills

- Coordinated and managed all aspects of more than 40 events sponsored by Student Activities Program Board.
- Organized structured training program related to all aspects of planning and executing events.
- Presented educational sessions relating to programming at regional conferences of the National Association for Campus Activities.
- Coordinated leadership seminars involving up to 70 students.
- Created special programs for fraternities and sororities based on chapter needs.

Advisory skills

- Advised Student Activities Program Board at community college, including contract negotiation, planning, event implementation, technical production, budgeting, critical thinking, ethics, and communication.
- Advised Greek council, a Panhellenic council, and members of five social fraternities and sororities in urban commuter university.
- Disciplined fraternities and sororities in accordance with university policies and procedures.
- Coordinated development of a university Panhellenic council.

Communication skills

- Prepared annual reports pertaining to positions held in higher education and private sector.
- Developed, administered, and interpreted results of annual commencement survey directed to more than 600 graduates.
- Developed, administered, and interpreted results of survey directed to 166 student organization presidents regarding leadership perceptions.
- Presented educational workshops on local, regional, and national levels to audiences of up to 150.

SUMMARY OF QUALIFICATIONS (cont.)

Management skills
- Managed budget of more than $150,000 and maintained accounts for commencement program board and capital outlays.
- Directed two chapter colonizations of social Greek organizations, including scheduling, advertising, recruiting student assistants, and public relations: increased membership 40% among organizations.
- Revised university policies concerning legal/fiscal relationships with Greek organizations.
- Hired, trained and supervised staff of 12 student workers and two clerical staff.
- Assisted in developing student activities mission statement at two institutions.

Editing skills
- Produced membership newsletter six times annually for 2,000 members of national professional fraternity.
- Prepared information packets for 34 student chapters, 41 chapter advisors, 12 alumni chapters, eight regional officers, and 10 national officers each quarter.
- Created and revised fraternity publications and manuals.

EMPLOYMENT HISTORY

Program Manager, College of Royal Oak, Royal Oak, Mich. (1993-1997)
Coordinator of Student Affairs, Madison College, Madison, Wis. (1988-1993)
Greek Advisor, University of Wisconsin at Milwaukee, Wis. (1987-1988)
Secondary Teacher, Indianapolis Public School System, Indianapolis, Ind. (1965-1986)

EDUCATION

Master's Degree in College Student Personnel Administration,
    University of Wisconsin at Milwaukee. with **highest honors** (1988)
Bachelor's Degree in Education, Indiana University, Bloomington (1965)

ACTIVITIES

Planning Committee, Fall Harvest Festival, Greenville, Mich. (1997-present)
Volunteer, Parkwood Nursing Home, Royal Oak, Mich. (1998-present)

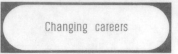
Mason J. Wheeler

855 Princeton Place
Wanatah, MN 55776
(218) 555-9223

Objective

A position as an insurance agent

Summary of Skills

- Licensed insurance agent in life, health and casualty.
- Experienced in working with insurance companies to develop employee benefit plans.
- Nearly 20 years management experience in private and public sector.
- Excellent interpersonal skills.

Work Experience

Deputy Director, Minnesota Emergency Medical Services Commission, Minneapolis, MN
(1997-present)
Manage and supervise office and field staff of 17. Maintain liaison with regional, state, and national agencies and organizations. Direct all agency programs and investigations.

- Administer state and federal grants and assist in preparing and managing agency budget.
- Consult with variety of insurance companies to enhance employee benefit plans.
- Established and implemented EMS regional coordination and quality assurance system, which raised standards of service provided.
- Developed Advanced Life Support Planning and Implementation Manual, which standardized procedures and equipment levels across the state.

Transportation Director, Minnesota Emergency Medical Services Commission, Minneapolis, MN
(1994-1997)
Administered transportation and disaster component of emergency medical services in State of Minnesota.

- Evaluated and approved all emergency medical services providers and vehicles for state certification.
- Developed regional emergency medical services, systems, transportation and disaster plans.
- Established Air Ambulance Standards for statewide implementation.

Work Experience

Administrative Assistant, Decatur County Memorial Hospital, Wanatah, MN
(1991-1994)
Handled general administration. Wrote grants and proposals.
• Directed Decatur County Emergency Medical Services.
• Assisted with event planning, public relations, and special projects.

Director of Decatur County Emergency Medical Services, Board of Commissioners of Decatur County, Wanatah, MN
(1988-1991)
Administered county emergency medical services. Trained, supervised, and hired/fired staff of 11 full-time (paid) and 60 part-time (volunteers) employees.
• Supervised maintenance of all ambulances in three county locations.
• Purchased materials and administered Medicare/Medicaid accounts.
• Handled budgeting, planning, public relations, and in-service/training activities.

Commissioner's Administrative Assistant, Decatur County Board of Commissioners, Wanatah, MN
(1984-1988)
• Served as liaison to board and county offices.
• Wrote and processed federal and state grants, loans, and policy proposals.
• Conducted computer study for county ambulance service and supervised conversion to computerized records.

Education/Licensing/Certification

Licensed Insurance Agent (2001)
M.S. in Public Administration, Minnesota University School of Public and
   Environmental Affairs, Lakeland (1987)
Certified Emergency Medical Technician (since 1965)
B.S. in Business Administration, Minnesota University, Lakeland (1964)

Activities

Director, Decatur County Parks & Recreation Board
Member, Decatur County Economic Development Planning Commission

Recently laid off

ANTHONY SALVATORE

458 E. Salisbury Lane
Willow, NY 10967
914·555·6768; 914·555·0412 (Cell phone)
TonySalvatore@mymail.net

SKILLS SUMMARY

Senior manager with extensive experience in site development. Skilled in securing federal, state, and local regulatory land-use approvals. Excellent background in facility design, construction, scheduling and budgeting. Experienced in developing and implementing regional and nationwide renovation programs for major organizations.

EMPLOYMENT

Senior Manager—Site Development, Truman &. Associates, Inc., Willow, NY (1992-2002)

➤ Managed due diligence requirements and governmental land-use approvals throughout the eastern United States for one of company's top accounts.

➤ Handled site selection and layout, defined design criteria, completed initial planning and cost estimates and secured funds.

➤ Coordinated and obtained all federal, state, and local regulatory land-use approvals.

➤ Interfaced with local planning, operating, finance, and legal organizations to meet local requirements and create positive relationship with community and civic leaders.

➤ Negotiated real estate documents and consultant contracts.

Senior Architectural Project Manager, Dothby's, Inc., Garden City, NJ (1985-1992)

➤ Handled complete design and construction coordination of company's retail facilities throughout the Northeastern United States and Atlantic Seaboard.

➤ Developed and implemented a nationwide remodel program for existing stores, which enhanced store operations, stock organization, and overall appearance.

Project Engineer, Corporate Real Estate Management, Atlantic Telephone & Electronics, Washington, DC (1980-1985)

➤ Managed design and construction of new buildings and renovations for office and equipment space at headquarters and in the field.

➤ Supervised and completed more than 40 projects in less than five years.

➤ Recommended and implemented new switching center design, which resulted in improved equipment maintenance and switching operations.

Facilities Design Engineer, Corporate Real Estate Management, Atlantic Telephone & Electronics, Washington, DC (1970-1980)

➤ Designed and provided cost estimates for new facilities.

➤ Recommended and implemented renovations program for out-of-date facilities, saving $20 million in new building costs.

EDUCATION

B.S. Civil Engineering, Pennsylvania State University, State College

Deborah K. Lyons
155 W. Tamarack Dr.
Batesville, AR. 72502
(501) 555-9293

Career goal Community Relations

Summary of experience

Organizational/management skills
+ Organized volunteers, secured corporate donations, and planned fund-raising events to pay for construction of $2 million Boys' and Girls' Club facility.
+ Serve on board of directors for club, help develop policies and procedures, and coordinate annual fund-raising auction, which provides more than $6,500 for operational expenses.
+ Recruited to supervise annual fund and membership drive for local library, raising donations 35% and membership 20% in two years.
+ Served two terms as secretary/treasurer of Parent/Teacher Association and recommended new parent/teacher conference idea that increased parent classroom participation 35%.
+ Managed three-member staff at rehabilitation hospital and increased productivity 25% despite operational changes brought on by two new owners in five years.

Communication/marketing skills
+ Work with local businesses and civic organizations to gain sponsors for 30 soccer, 40 basketball, and 25 baseball teams.
+ Developed brochure to attract and retain club members and sponsors.
+ Handle publicity for local March of Dimes walk-a-thon, which has seen participation increase 35% and donations increase 40% over the last three years.
+ Handled three in-house, high-volume accounts for rehabilitation hospital and helped develop long-term marketing plan that increased number of clients 25%.

Instructional skills
+ Supervised Arkansas Dyslexic Association's Saturday math program for more than 300 students and tutored up to 30 hours per week.
+ Developed new tour guide program for local hospital and trained up to 15 volunteer tour guides.

Experience Fund-raising Chairperson, Batesville Public Library (2001-present)
Director, Fund-raising Chairperson, Batesville Boys' and Girls' Club (1999-present)
Local Publicity Chairman, March of Dimes Walk-a-thon (1997-present)
Volunteer, Wishard Memorial Hospital, Batesville, Ark. (1998-1999)
Secretary/Treasurer, Parent/Teacher Association,
    Tipton County Community School Corp. (1996-1998)
Volunteer, Arkansas Dyslexic Association, Little Rock (1995-1998)
Admissions Director, McKenzie Hospitals, Little Rock (1990-1995)
LPN, McKenzie Hospitals, Little Rock (1988-1990)
LPN, Robert W. Hall, M.D., Batesville (1987-1988)

SANDRA W. RICHARDSON
39 Citation Circle
Ames, IA 50602
(319) 555-6887
SandyRich@mailuser.net

CAREER OBJECTIVE   Secondary School Teacher

SKILLS SUMMARY   Manager, engineer, and instructor with extensive background in operations, leadership, instruction, and training. Demonstrated ability to successfully train and lead up to 1,800-person unit. Solid education in instructional techniques. Licensed teacher in the state of Iowa.

EDUCATION   Iowa State University, Ames (1998-2001)
➤ Master of Education

Iowa State University, Ames (1994-1997)
➤ Undergraduate courses to fulfill teaching certificate requirements

U.S. Military Academy, West Point, NY (1984)
➤ Bachelor of Science in Engineering

PROFESSIONAL STUDIES   Officer Basic and Advanced Course (1986)
➤ 18-month post-graduate schooling that included lesson plan preparation, instruction, and training techniques.

Combined Arms Staff College (1987)
➤ Senior officer schooling focusing on staff and administrative functions and covering advanced briefing and instructional techniques.

LICENSING   Secondary Education Teaching Certificate - State of Iowa (1997)

INSTRUCTIONAL EXPERIENCE
1998-present   **Substitute Teacher, Ames Public School System, Ames, Iowa**
Complete a variety of assignments, including 12-week assignment in high school biology and chemistry classes.
➤ Created special unit for history curriculum on Desert Storm and its significance in U.S. military history.

**INSTRUCTIONAL
EXPERIENCE**

1990-1993   **Operations Manager, U.S. Army, Dhahran, Saudi Arabia**
Handled all operations and training of 1,800-person logistics unit
that provided supplies for Middle East. Tour of duty included
Operation Desert Storm.
➤ Unit commended by General Schwartzkopf.
➤ Demonstrated ability to rapidly create and execute team
training program under demanding conditions.

1989-1990   **Commander, U.S. Army, West Germany**
Managed 150-person unit.
➤ Administered training program that effectively taught individual,
collective, and multi-echelon (various level of command) skills to
produce a combat-ready unit.

1985-1989   **Training Officer, U.S. Army, California and West Germany**
Served as training supervisor for 125-person unit and training
manager for 500-person unit.
➤ Handled hands-on teaching and curriculum development.
➤ Created alternative means of assessment, which more accurately
identified accomplishments and areas needing improvement.

1984   **Cadet Basic Training Squad Leader and Platoon Leader,
U.S. Military Academy, West Point, NY**
Taught and led unique and exciting eight-week educational
experience.
➤ Served on team that transformed a culturally and educationally
diverse freshman class into a cohesive group of young men and
women, prepared for rigors of cadet life.

ACTIVITIES   Volunteer Tutor, Carnegie Public Library, Ames, Iowa
Girl Scout Leader, Troop 121, Ames, Iowa

EDWARD T. FIELDS

105 Magnolia Dr.   (904) 555-1664
Talagusa, FL 32302   EdFields@mycomp.net

Skills Profile

Nearly 10 years of aeronautical and engineering experience, including obtaining five
commercial and experimental patents. Skilled in developing methods that have become
Air Force standards. Solid background in computer and software operations, budget
and personnel management, and training.

Work Experience

Air Force Flight Test Center, Samuels Air Force Base, FL (1996-present)

Captain/Flight Commander, 1998-present

Program manager for testing and evaluating integrated software systems
on F-15 aircraft. F-15 airborne test director and weapon system operator.

- Managed schedule and costs within budget of approximately $14M per year.
- Supervised 17 engineers and three technicians, wrote performance evaluations, and
  oversaw training.
- Saved $120K in annual costs through cross-training.
- Developed original methods for weapons accuracy analysis, which was published and
  presented at professional conference and recommended for Air Force standard.

Captain/Lead Avionics Engineer, 1996-1998

Prepared technical and safety flight test plans, reviewed and approved
technical reports of test results and authorized specific flight profiles.

- Directed hazardous, low-level flight program with no safety incidents.
- Wrote published standards of radar altimeter suitability as test data source.
- Implemented computerized data base to control aircraft software configuration.

Shuttle Test Group, Williams Air Force Base, CA (1991-1993)

Lieutenant/Mechanisms Engineer

Served with unit providing Air Force support for Space Shuttle operations.

- Console-certified engineer for pre-launch processing and launch operations.
- Member of Kennedy Space Center launch control room team for four launches.

Education   United States Air Force Test Pilot School, Williams Air Force Base, CA (1996)
                      Air Force Institute of Technology, Dayton, OH (1995)
                      - Masters of Science in Aeronautical Engineering
                      - Awarded joint patent on experimental nozzle design
                      Syracuse University, Syracuse, New York (1991)
                      - Bachelor of Arts in Engineering Science
                      - Received joint patent on commercial electro-mechanical design

Current Status   Captain, United States Air Force Reserve (Clearance: Secret)

Awards   2000 Outstanding Volunteer, Talagusa Girls' and Boys' Club

Activities   Volunteer/Basketball Coach, Talagusa Girls' and Boys' Club (1998-pesent)
                      Project Leader, Eagle Scout Radio-Controlled Airplane project (1998-present)

GREAT OCCUPATIONAL RESUMES

The occupational resumes in this chapter are good models for many of the same reasons those in Chapter 4 were so effective: They are concise and clear. They address the *employer's* needs. They present quantifiable results. And they list *specific* accomplishments.

The sample situational resumes featured a broad range of occupations, from aeronautical engineer to sports reporter, architect to veterinarian, bank vice president to music teacher. But here are 66 more covering just as wide a range, from "basic" careers like accountant, nurse and teacher to the more specialized, like community outreach manager, gymnastics instructor, and legislative assistant.

Accountant   **117**

Gwen (p. 117) and Monica ("tax accountant," p. 204) are both accountants, but Gwen emphasizes her cost accounting and auditing experience while Monica stresses her tax accounting and benefits-planning achievements. Gwen also lists her computer skills immediately after her Summary, to draw attention to her broad knowledge of accounting software. Both include supportive volunteer work.

Administrative assistant   **119**

Even though Elaine has solid work experience, she still includes her previous volunteer work and vocational schooling to further illustrate how she has used and developed her skills. Her Summary of Qualifications includes a surprising number of facts, from her lengthy experience (11 years) and specific skills (word processing, accounting software, telephone, filing) to specific experience (handling confidential information) and general skills (meeting deadlines, interpersonal, and organizational).

Airline maintenance technician   **120**

Anyone seeking such a worker will have very specific requirements, and Scott makes sure his combination resume includes every detail in terms the employer will understand and appreciate (even if we don't). Because the specific types of aircraft and engines Scott has worked on is the most important information, this section is fully 60 percent of his resume. A prospective employer will look to see where he's done all this, but only after concluding he has exactly the right experience.

Auto mechanic   121

Because they are directly related to his career, Patrick includes specific high school courses (even though he has graduated from a vocational college) and a "Related Interest." I particularly like the use of the word "related."

His Skill Summary does an excellent job of defining the kinds of vehicles on which he has worked, specific systems on which he is experienced, the functions he regularly performs—even the kind of tools with which he is familiar.

Bank branch manager   122

Marianne lets her experience do the talking for her, though you wouldn't immediately notice that all of it has been at a single bank, most of it at a single branch. Nevertheless, by zeroing in on key accomplishments, she ably supports her tightly written Profile. Notice that she includes her high school graduation because she never attended college (though she also, of course, includes her coursework at the National Banking Institute, clearly demonstrating the drive that helped her rise from teller to branch manager in less than a decade).

Business analyst   123

Margaret's Profile neatly summarizes a targeted career at a single company. It can be as "general" as it is—"solid business background," "sound business decisions," "deliver on time and at or below budget"—because of the highly specific accomplishments she lists for each career step. Although she has an advanced degree, her work experience is more important in her particular field, so she places it first.

Business office director   124

While Omkar has solid, results-oriented experience, he also highlights his advanced degree, certification, and involvement in professional organizations to support his work history.

For those of you who despaired when I suggested you write *a series* of targeted resumes, consider what Omkar would do if he were *not* seeking a job at another hospital or similar facility. His Profile would need to be radically altered, but otherwise (with the possible exception of eliminating the professional organizations), the rest of his resume could remain virtially unchanged.

Carpenter   125

Ronald's employment background is varied, but he does a nice job of crafting a clear, targeted Objective, summarizing skills pertinent to it, then detailing construction-related accomplishments to support it. He also includes activities that are clearly related to his career goal.

Civil/construction management engineer   126

Elisabeth has the luxury of featuring job titles that, with no further explanation, clearly illustrate her steadily increasing ability to handle responsibility. Notice the common language and structure of the first bullet under each of her three most recent positions (with the same company). Again, this alone demonstrates the growth of her abilities—from managing projects with budgets of $5.5 million to

$20 million to $135 million and dimensions from small (and unmentioned) to 1,500 parking spaces to 520,000 square feet. She even manages to quantity results under Memberships!

Commodity/transportation specialist 128

Brian has a somewhat unusual career but describes his responsibilities and highlights his achievements in laymen's terms. He uses numbers to quantify his results and clearly explains his contributions to successful business expansion. Like many of the resumes in this chapter, he has eliminated extraneous information from his resume—just a Profile, Career History, and one-line Education section.

Community outreach manager 130

Janet highlights her nursing degree first, then her experience in establishing successful outreach programs, including her (highly valued) ability to work with government agencies. She uses power words throughout the detailed listings of her accomplishments: "established," "created," "supervised," "developed," "initiated."

Community parks director 132

In short bullets, Jeanne highlights the three things she wants a prospective employer to notice: 8 years experience, background in facilities management, administrator with fund-raising and budget-management skills. While she adds extensive, results-oriented details when describing her park-related jobs, the entry for her teaching job is much shorter, though it highlights the one accomplishment that is directly career-related. She also makes sure to include her career-related minor in the Education section.

Computer programmer 133

With most resumes, it's important to use simple language, but high-tech jobs present a problem. Sometimes the work is so specialized that technical information *can't* be translated into laymen's terms. If you're in a high-tech field, prospective employers will certainly understand the language, but many non-technical human resources people may be lost.

Sara has solid experience, but she makes sure to list the computer languages and platforms she has mastered *first*, in order to immediately communicate the breadth of her knowledge. She then uses the Employment section to emphasize specific accomplishments. Both the school she attended and her *cum laude* credential are impressive enough to highlight, but her degree is not pertinent to her current job. As a result, she keeps her brief Education entry at the end of her resume.

Computer software specialist 134

Linda is in a highly specialized area—to fully explain her accomplishments in laymen's terms would take five pages. Since most prospective employers she'll be contacting *aren't* laymen, she utilizes the appropriate technical language. Linda supports her qualifications with an impressive list of publications, awards, and patent information.

Corporate communications professional 136

In a tightly written Profile, Thomas summarizes his well-rounded background in most aspects of corporate communications. He then highlights major accomplishments at each job, quantifying results throughout. He cites professional awards to support his Profile's very first claim.

Cosmetologist/salon manager 138

Jamie's combination resume nicely summarizes her abilities, making it easy for any employer to immediately see the products she's worked with and the specialized training she's received. But her Summary also draws attention to her sales promotion, customer service, purchasing, and inventory management experience. This is clearly someone ready to take the next step up the career ladder.

Counselor/therapist 139

Everything on Rebecca's impressive resume is career-related, including her extensive Volunteer Experience, Education, Certifications, even her Memberships. This "generic" resume should be used if she seeks a similar job at a larger hospital or facility. But if she decides to concentrate on a single area of counseling—substance abuse, eating disorders, domestic violence—her varied background will not be as much of a strength. In that case, she should utilize a functional resume to more explicitly highlight her skills and expertise in one particular area.

Dance instructor 141

Victoria highlights her ability to place students with major dance troupes and coordinate fund raising and special promotions. She also includes significant details of her own performing experience and education to lend weight to her accomplishments. Since with whom one studies is highly important in any of the arts, she lists teachers for each general dance area.

Daycare attendant 143

Laura's resume reveals that she's gaining career-related experience and initiating new programs while pursuing an associate's degree. She includes her GPA to show how successfully she has juggled several responsibilities simultaneously. Everything about her resume proclaims that she's ready to take on more responsibility.

Dental assistant 144

Susan summarizes her specific skills right up front, then lists her employment chronologically. She also makes sure to point out that she managed an "A" average in trade school while still finishing high school *and* working part-time in her field *and* being honored—twice—as a top dental assistant.

Disc jockey 145

Christopher's resume clearly states results-oriented accomplishments and shows his community involvement. Note that he includes his GPA and work at his vocational school's radio station in his list of achievements. Including the latter adds immensely to his "experienced" claim, since he's only been out of school a short time.

Dispatcher/driver manager 146

Nathan managed to seamlessly transform himself from an Air Force medical technician to a dispatcher responsible for a relatively large fleet. He doesn't downplay his time in the military because it provided him with so much supervisory experience, which he has since put to use in an entirely new field. This would also be an excellent resume for him to use if he decided to change fields again.

Electrical engineer   **147**

Gary manages to communicate an extensive background in a highly technical field in words even I can understand! He also does an excellent job of using numbers to support his accomplishments—from cost savings to increased profit margins to budget responsibilities.

Both his advisory position with the Association of Student Engineers and his work with the 4-H club are the kinds of "extra value" activities enlightened employers look for.

Environmental education/recreation management   **149**

Anna's Skills Summary certainly doesn't indicate she has yet to graduate from college. It would definitely make *me* read on, and doing so would reveal an individual focused on a specific career with the education (note the inclusion of pertinent courses) and volunteer experience to back her up. Anna includes both "fluent in Spanish" and her work with the museum in an effort to add even more value.

Executive administrator   **150**

Although Carol (p. 150) uses virtually the same format as Elaine (an administrative assistant, see p. 119), she has substituted "Professional Experience" for Elaine's "Work Experience," a subtle but advisable change. Her Summary of Qualifications is concise but value-packed, and she's done an excellent job of detailing 10 years of increasing responsibility in a single-page resume.

Exercise scientist/occupational rehabilitation   **151**

It's not always possible nor advisable to translate technical skills into laymen's terms—anyone perusing Jeffrey's resume should know what "Valhalla Medical 1990B Bio-Impedance" is. After he's defined the specific tests/functions and machines he's familiar with, his Experience section highlights his administrative, training, and organizational skills. His entire resume is completely focused.

Fire chief   **153**

Kent's resume stresses his ability to develop and implement innovative public-safety programs, but it also highlights the management and organizational skills that would easily help him transition into the corporate job market. His Activities and Awards reveal his commitment to his community.

Food services manager   **155**

Wendy highlights her experience with budgets and people, both essential skills in her chosen field. Her bulleted Summary of Qualifications utilizes key words to communicate experience, ability, and required skills. Clearly wishing to continue her career climb, she uses a variety of statistics to illustrate her ability to take on even more responsibility.

Graphic artist/video producer   **156**

After a well-drafted Summary, Tim details his experience with the specific computer programs and systems endemic to his field. He then profiles his skills and talents with results-oriented achievements. The resume's simple design helps draw one's eye to its major divisions, making even the Awards stand out, as well they should.

Gymnastics instructor 158

"Champion." What a great first word for a prospective employer to see! And the rest of Natalie's resume supports it—clearly describing someone who has transformed herself from a, yes, champion gymnast into a respected coach and experienced instructor.

Human resources professional 159

Justin began his career in the military but successfully transitioned into a similar position in the civilian job market. He has continued to achieve quantified results and highlights his innovative contributions. Note that he also includes a career-related military honor.

Insurance manager 160

Gary communicates extensive experience in personnel and product management and emphasizes his ability to assume positions with increasing responsibility. He includes his college credit hours, even though they were earned some time ago, in an attempt to downplay the fact that he is only a high school graduate.

Interior designer 162

Leslie is an experienced designer who owns her own business. Although most of her clients come to her by word of mouth, she's compiled a resume to present to potential clients. She highlights her specialized skills in restaurant planning and design—where she now gets the bulk of her business—but includes achievements in residential design to show her well-rounded background (and potentially attract non-restaurant customers).

Legislative assistant 164

As a legislative assistant, John is constantly working within the community and highlights his ability to determine and address local concerns and issues. He also indicates his experience in event planning and fund raising, both relevant skills in his field. He's so "numbers-oriented" that he even cites the quantity of pages he had to analyze during his internship.

Librarian 165

Five bullets. Five distinct areas of skill and expertise. Five reasons any library director should give this resume a thorough read. That's what a Summary should accomplish, and Elizabeth's clearly does. Does she still want to be a children's librarian? Given her first bullet, it would certainly seem so. But if she were ready to move into a different area or attempt to move up to a library directorship, simply substituting two other achievements/skills for her first and third bullets would certainly work.

Loan manager 167

Government employees need to stress their ability to work within the system (a prime requirement for *any* government job!) but may also have to emphasize how those and other skills could apply within the civilian job market.

Dennis currently works as an agricultural lender for a government agency, but he's interested in a job as a bank loan officer. In his Summary, he states his experience in public administration and with government contracts, but his achievements emphasize his ability to develop and manage secure loan packages.

Maintenance supervisor   **169**

You probably wouldn't expect Greg to utilize such a combination resume, but it does an excellent job of drawing attention to the equipment and tools with which he is familiar, which is more important than where he wielded them. Notice how the single accomplishment under his military service is career-related and how he has managed to include his responsibility for an innovative idea at each of the jobs he has held.

Manufacturing manager   **170**

Timothy profiles his strengths in facility, personnel, and production management and uses action words to communicate his leadership abilities. I think "Career History" has a nicer "ring" than the mundane "Employment" or "Work Experience."

Marketing director   **171**

Claire's resume emphasizes an all-around background in a variety of healthcare areas, showing her ability to "wear all hats," from public relations to contract negotiation. Given that her Profile emphasizes her experience in the *industry* as opposed to marketing (her latest title), this resume may be her attempt to move higher in hospital administration.

Marketing manager   **172**

Yee Su manages to include quite a lot of pertinent results-specific information in her tightly written resume. This kind of resume gives the impression that its writer is just "giving the facts" and is ready to go into much greater detail during the interview—so let's set an appointment!

Materials engineer   **174**

Jeanette has an extensive educational background and highlights her theses and publications to further emphasize her areas of specialty and knowledge. She makes sure to include her doctorate in the first sentence of her Profile, but follows it immediately with her project management experience. This is the resume of someone ready to move to the next level.

Medical transcriptionist   **176**

Although Michael hasn't completed a formal degree, he includes related vocational training and stresses his computer software and excellent typing skills, all of which many employers would require for his position. But he also highlights managerial skills, including cutting expenses and establishing successful office management policies, in an attempt to stand out from the crowd.

Nonprofit agency director   **177**

Theresa built her nonprofit agency from scratch and uses figures to quantify her achievements. She adds more details about her teaching job than one would normally expect, but they are solid accomplishments that tie in to her new career.

Nurse   **179**

Rhonda profiles her ability to develop specific, patient-related programs and provide award-winning care. She does an excellent job detailing the many varied duties she had at each level of her career. Notice she also includes her student extern experience.

Office manager 181

Susan uses bulleted, detailed, results-oriented accomplishments to stress the office management skills she's developed after starting at the bottom of the career totem pole. She also makes sure to note extra vocational courses that are pertinent to her career.

Operations manager 182

Cynthia manages to include a plethora of targeted information in a relatively simple, single-page resume. Nevertheless, a prospective employer would be hard pressed not to conclude that she is a winner.

Paralegal 183

Sandra's Certifications are most important, so she lists them after an excellent Summary of her skills. The clean, crisp design of her resume allows her to include a surprising amount of pertinent information on a single page.

Pharmacist 184

While Amanda doesn't downplay her pharmacological experience with government agencies (how could she?), she certainly goes out of her way to stress her managerial skills. She even manages to shoehorn "consultant" into her summary. Could she be seeking a job in the private sector? This resume would certainly be a first step.

Production control manager 186

Miguel has been a manager for a relatively short time, but he indicates how his extensive production background prepared and provided him with the necessary skills and knowledge to advance. Note his use of numbers to quantify results. Although he has no formal degree, he includes related studies to complement his achievements. Simply noting that he is an Eagle Scout Leader is an attempt to do everything possible to accentuate his leadership experience (and downplay its brevity).

Public information director 188

Douglas has a solid background in public information and emphasizes his skill and experience developing and implementing unique programs. He also outlines his editorial experience and includes continuing education courses to complement his state agency experience.

Public relations professional 190

Though some may consider her Skills Summary a little long, or prefer that she use bullets to highlight her many claims to fame, it certainly covers every base. Susana emphasizes her recent advanced degree by listing it before the Experience section. She supports a results-oriented resume with a list of the significant contributions she has made to pertinent professional organizations.

Quality manager 192

In a simple format, Edward is able to emphasize his accomplishments in manufacturing and quality control and profile his ability to assume increased responsibility through the significant (and quantified) contributions he's already made on the job.

Quality review auditor   **193**

Christina's resume shows steady advancement in the same field (almost for the same company) in a relatively short period of time. Given her emphasis of "the insurance field" in her summary, it is likely she is seeking to move to a higher level at a similar company. In a tightly written, single-page format, she highlights the achievements that brought her to her current position. Since her limited college courses were directly career-related, she makes sure to include them.

Restaurant manager   **194**

Randall, a restaurant manager, uses a slightly different format to highlight significant achievements in employee and service management. He uses numbers wherever possible, from describing the size of the restaurants he's managed to the specific savings and increased profit margins he's achieved. He also includes a management-training program in his Education listing to add weight to his relatively limited management experience. The last sentence of his Skills Summary is a gem.

Sales—agricultural   **195**

Though a trifle long, Michael's Skills Summary should certainly pique the interest of any employer seeking someone with his background. Like Theresa (see next resume), he has included numerous statistics to back up his contentions, but he has also bulleted accomplishments to support his assertion of supervisory and production management experience.

Sales—computer systems   **197**

While I've counseled all of you to quantify results wherever possible, sales professionals *must* include pertinent numbers and percentages—the more, the better—as Theresa does. But she also prominently displays her computer skills (right under the Skills Summary) and includes two activities to show she has outside interests…that are directly related to her career. Note how facts about her awards are seamlessly integrated into her bulleted sections.

Sales—retail   **199**

Tammy's bulleted Skills Profile effectively describes her abilities, and the way she has constructed her Employment History backs her up. She includes her high school education because she did not attend college, but draws little attention to it—it's not bold-faced.

School superintendant   **200**

As a school superintendent, Kevin has a solid background in implementing innovative school programs, and he briefly, yet clearly, highlights his achievements. His professional activities relate his experience with a variety of educational organizations, and his community service shows he's a well-rounded individual. He lists his many educational reform presentations on a separate sheet (not shown).

Small business owner (seeking investors)   **202**

Kenneth's resume was compiled to attract prospective investors. His resume makes it apparent that he has established strong roots in a single community (Bozeman, Montana), both through his business and other activities. And those activities perfectly complement his business. Given his goal, he makes sure to accentuate his already successful attempts to enhance sales through expansion.

Social worker 203

Nancy's Summary of Qualifications packs a lot of punch, covering her experience (in some detail) and talents in five concise but informative sentences. Her job titles alone show the arc of her career, so I wouldn't be surprised if this resume had been prepared so she can take the next step. Note the important inclusion of her double major while in college.

Tax accountant 204

Monica also uses five sentences in her Summary of Qualifications. In her case, I like the use of bullets, which helps the short sentences stand out but doesn't allow the important, but very long, fourth sentence to get lost. She does a nice job of mixing brief descriptions of her duties and responsibilities, meaningful accomplishments, and quantified results. And her extensive "Activities" are so career-related as to demand listing under "Professional Affiliations."

Teacher—elementary school 206

Teacher—secondary school 208

Teachers may want to include an Objective to identify the specific areas in which they wish to teach. Beginning teachers should include their student teaching experiences. All teachers should list licensing information.

Abigail currently is teaching third grade, but she is licensed for kindergarten through third grade. To keep her options open, she includes all levels in her Objective. Louise chose not to include an Objective because her Skills Profile and most recent job title clearly indicate her specialty.

Notice how both teachers summarize their general teaching skills in their Profiles and emphasize their achievements in their Employment sections. Abigail is quite involved outside the classroom and includes her many educational and instructional activities to convey her interests and her ability to handle several responsibilities.

Technical software director 210

Marissa is in a more generalized area than some of our other "high-tech" job-seekers and can therefore "gear down" the technical language. While she has a strong work history, she puts her Education first to emphasize her MBA. Notice her well-stated and quantified results.

Training manager 212

In only three sentences, Rosa manages to convey her ability to manage programs and client relations plus her "extensive experience" in both insurance and marketing. It's important that she noted the management and training courses that supplement her marketing degree and perfectly tie in with the trajectory of her career.

Writer 214

Lisa's resume trumpets her ability to tailor information to specific groups and lead related workshops. Her Skills Summary communicates not just experience ("10 years") but *broad* experience ("wide range of subject matter"), allowing her to use the same resume for a greater variety of writing jobs.

GWEN H. INGRAM
438 South Street
Camden, Utah 84776
(801) 555-2242
GHIngram@alo.com

SKILLS SUMMARY   Certified Public Accountant with seven years experience, specializing in cost accounting. Skilled in analyzing data, performing audits, and examining internal control procedures. Solid background in, and knowledge of, financial accounting systems.

COMPUTER SKILLS   Lotus, Excel, Ami Pro, WordPerfect, ProComm Plus, Spreadsheet Auditor, Flowcharting III, and Focaudit.

ACCOUNTING EXPERIENCE

2000-present   **Senior Accountant/Analyst**
Western Mutual-Medicare
Salt Lake City, Utah
Determine reimbursable costs payable to providers of medical care under the Medicare program.
✦ Analyze financial and statistical data submitted on provider cost reports.
✦ Review current and fixed assets, liabilities, charges, revenue, and expenses.
✦ Compile statistical data for the basis of allocation of indirect costs.
✦ Prepare audit adjustment reports.
✦ Initiated and implemented new provider pricing policies, which established consistency in charges.

1996-2000   **Staff Auditor—Corporate Trust, Operations and Retail Lending**
First Bank and Trust
Salt Lake City, Utah
Performed financial, operational, regulatory compliance, and system-integrated audits. Trained and supervised work of assigned staff.
✦ Conducted examinations of internal control procedures, which led to improved financial accounting operations.
✦ Prepared audit reports and developed recommendations for bank officers and bank management.
✦ Assisted in pre-acquisition audits of purchased banks to determine financial condition, leading to successful business expansion.

OTHER EXPERIENCE

1995-1996
Loan Officer
Citizens' Trust
Camden, Utah
Developed, originated, documented, and closed commercial, consumer, and mortgage loans, concentrating in residential construction lending.
+ Served on team that developed and implemented new policies and procedures involving commercial lending, resulting in higher customer satisfaction.
+ Developed and implemented indirect lending program, which filled a need as identified by customer feedback.

1993-1995
Loan Processor
Citizens Trust
Camden, Utah
Assisted loan officer in documenting and closing commercial, consumer, and mortgage loans.
+ Member of team that doubled mortgage turnover in two years.

EDUCATION
University of Utah, Salt Lake City
+ 12 credit hours in Continuing Education in Accounting (1999-2000)
+ Bachelor of Science in Business Administration (1993)

LICENSING
Certified Public Accountant (1996)

ACTIVITIES
Member, Camden Community Band
Planning Committee, Camden Fourth of July Festival
Treasurer, Kappa Kappa Kappa philanthropic organization

Elaine Godfrey • 901 E. Vine St. • Huntington, MO • 65326 • (816) 555-5423 • Godfrey@mail.net

Summary of Qualifications

Eleven years providing office administrative and clerical support, including handling confidential information. Skilled in word processing and accounting software, including Lotus 1-2-3 and WordPerfect. Accustomed to meeting tight deadlines. Excellent telephone, filing, interpersonal, and organizational skills. Experienced in meeting planning and travel arrangements.

Work Experience

Administrative Assistant, PowerPlay, Inc., St. Louis, MO (1997 - present)
- Schedule monthly meetings and handle travel arrangements for 17 field and regional headquarters staff members; prepare all necessary paperwork and audio/visual materials; make meal and hotel arrangements; process travel expense reports.
- Prepare all correspondence, invoices, and administrative reports for department manager.
- Track budget and prepare quarterly reports.
- Implemented Electronic Mail system for field staff, resulting in faster communication and quicker responses to headquarters's requests.
- Trained clerical staff in accounting computer software, saving outside training expenses of $2,000.

Senior Clerk, PowerPlay, Inc., St. Louis. MO (1995 - 1997)
- Provided clerical support for secretarial and associate staff.
- Prepared all department's computerized graphs, charts, and visual presentation aids.
- Standardized department filing system so secretarial staff could easily locate information in any filing center

Records Clerk, Huntington Home Bank, Huntington, MO (1993 - 1995)
- Recorded and filed employee benefit, salary, and annual evaluation information.
- Assisted with payroll preparation and entered data on keypunch machine.
- Served as liaison between computer room and payroll supervisor and managed delivery and pick-up of confidential information.
- Sponsored department's participation in community walk-a-thon fund drive; department won highest participation award and third-highest per-capita donation award.

Volunteer Experience

Church Secretary, Huntington United Methodist Church, Huntington, MO (1992 - 1993)
- Prepared all written communication, answered telephones and prepared weekly bulletins.
- Designed and implemented Master Schedule and User Guidelines for church and community meetings and weddings, which reduced scheduling conflicts and building maintenance costs.

Education

Owen Tech Vocational School, Salisbury, MO (1992 - 1993)
- Computer Operations
- Business Communication
- Office Management

Airline maintenance technician

Scott Davis

501 N. Jackson Ave. • Akron, CO • 80113 • (303) 555-9203 • SDavis@mailstar.net

Summary of Skills

General

- Perform "C" check maintenance on Boeing 757, Boeing 727 (200 and 100 series aircraft) and L1011 Tristar.
- Complete regular 100-hour and annual inspections of aircraft, including Piper Navajo, DC 3, Beech Craft 18, and Cessna 150/180.
- Handle regular inspection, compression checks, and maintenance of Continental, Lycoming, Pratt and Whitney 1830/2000, and Wright 1820 engines, along with composite repairs.

Composite

- Experienced with RB211 core cowls 72-03-01.
- Skilled with build-up repair on spoilers on L1011.
- Experienced with Honeycomb sandwich repair due to delamination 51-50-07.
- Completed the following work on 727:
  - alodine & prime 51-10-2
  - corrosion removal 51-10-6
  - fastener installation 51-30-2
  - typical formed section 51-40-3
  - fiberglass overlays 51-40-8
- Completed the following work on L1011:
  - alodine & prime 51-21-02
  - corrosion removal 51-21-01
  - fastener installation 51-40-00A
  - typical rib or former repair 51-50-03
  - rub strips 51-50-11

Employment History

Airline Maintenance Technician, AmWest Airlines, Denver International Airport, Denver, CO (2000-present)

- Service and handle preventive maintenance on commercial aircraft for regional airline.
- Served on team to re-evaluate duties and review maintenance checklist, resulting in new procedures that increased productivity and reduced overlapping responsibilities.

Airline Mechanic, Combs Air Maintenance, Denver International Airport, Denver, CO (1998-2000)

- Served as key member of two-man aircraft maintenance and inspection service while attending Lamont University.
- Serviced private and corporate aircraft under direct supervision of an A and P certified mechanic.

Education

A.S. in Aviation Maintenance Technology, Lamont University (1999)
Additional certification in FAR 65 airframe and power plant mechanics (2001)

PATRICK HENNESSEY
1593 Oak St.
Galesburg, AR 72847
(501) 555-3922

SUMMARY OF SKILLS

- Skilled in repair and maintenance of automobiles, vans, and trucks, with advanced skills in diesel repair and maintenance.
- Strong background in working with cooling, air-conditioning, electrical, fuel, exhaust, and steering systems.
- Experienced in tire rotation, rotor resurfacing, bearing replacement, and front-end alignment.
- Skilled with all gauges, wrenches, and machine, air, and hand tools.
- Experienced in diagnosing performance problems, writing accurate work orders, and preparing estimates.

PROFESSIONAL EXPERIENCE

2000-present

Automotive Mechanic, Goodyear Tire and Repair Service, Galesburg, Ark.

- Successfully diagnose and repair an average of 10 vehicles per week.
- Handle all diesel repairs.
- Designed new work order form on shop's computer system, resulting in easier access for all mechanics (versus previous manual system where orders could easily be misfiled) and easier retrieval for billing/accounting purposes.

1998-2000

Automotive Mechanic, Shelby Chevrolet, Hockessin, Ark.

- Handled repair and maintenance of domestic cars and trucks.
- Ran and maintained the lube rack.
- Recommended use of a new lubricant, which produced superior results at half the cost of previous lubricant.

EDUCATION/ TRAINING

1997

Graduate, Hockessin High School, Hockessin, Ark.

- Related course work: Automotive Shop, Advanced Auto Shop, Computer Operations

1997-1998

Truman Career Vocational College, Waverly, Ark.

- Completed curriculum and certification in automotive repair
- Completed additional certification in diesel repair
- Finished second in graduating class

RELATED INTEREST

- Build re-creations of vintage sports cars

MARIANNE G. LISTER
45 E. Main St.
Waterloo, OR 97236
(503) 555-2093; (503) 555-1101
Marianne@quick.net

Profile:
Extensive management experience and comprehensive banking background. Skilled in establishing new branch offices, policies, and procedures. Experienced in developing investment and brokerage services.

Work Experience:

2000-current
Branch Manager, Society National Bank, Portland, OR
Supervise branch operations, new account personnel and investment department. Train all new employees.
➤ Guided branch through successful conversion to new computer system, products, and procedures, resulting in enhanced customer service, more accessible records, and better account report generation.
➤ Successfully established policy and procedures governing membership of the bank in the Portland Clearing House, Federal Reserve, Portland.

1997-2000
Assistant Manager, Society National Bank (formerly Home National Bank), Eugene, OR
Supervised daily branch operations, including teller line and new accounts. Managed vault operations. Trained new tellers.
➤ Managed buying/selling of currency for seven-branch network.
➤ Successfully established the bank's first branch office in the Portland market, creating new business opportunities for the bank, a new employer for the community, and enhanced customer services.

1994-1997
Investment Officer, Home National Bank, Eugene, OR
Sold CDs, Treasury Bills/Bonds, U.S. Bonds, IRAs/QRPs and served as a discount broker.
➤ Established new IRA procedures and the bank's Discount Brokerage Service, expanding customer service offerings and creating new businesses for the bank.

1991-1994
Teller, Home National Bank, Eugene, OR
Handled teller duties, assisted in safe deposit box area and served as backup to loan, new account, and investment departments.
➤ Successfully balanced branch's daily records.
➤ Recommended new procedure for businesses making large Monday morning deposits, enhancing service for those business customers and eliminating wait for personal account customers.

Education/Training:
National Banking Institute, Eugene, OR (1992-1994)
➤ Courses in investment banking, discount brokerage services, and loan processing and monitoring
Graduate, Mantooth Memorial High School, Big Bend, OR (1991)

MARGARET SCHUETTE

1021 Miller Ct. • Columbus, OH • 43298 • (614) 555-6304 • MSchuette@mail.net

SKILLS PROFILE
- Solid background in business analysis and long-range strategic planning.
- Skilled in leading teams of diverse backgrounds to make sound business decisions based on analyses of short- and long-term business needs.
- Able to take a large conceptual problem or project, break it into components, establish plans and a critical path, achieve incremental goals, and deliver project on time and at or below budget.

PROFESSIONAL EXPERIENCE

North America AgChem, Columbus, OH
Sr. Business Analyst (2001-present)
Work cross-functionally with marketing, manufacturing, research and development, legal, and finance to balance product lines and determine business strategy.
- Established new financial analysis procedure for marketing plans, which has redirected more than $5 million in unprofitable marketing expenditures to more productive areas, such as product development.
- Restructured portfolio for research group, which provides guidelines for determining company funding for current and future projects and aids in long-range budgeting and business planning.
- Serve as controller for $162 million agricultural chemical product group.

Sr. Contract Manufacturing Administrator (1998-2001)
Led teams of various disciplines, such as sales, scientific, and manufacturing staffs, in problem-solving, cost planning, and quality control of various products.
- Successfully managed formulation of $31.5 million agricultural products at third-party manufacturing sites across the country.
- Developed long-range strategy for agricultural chemical product, which fully utilized in-house capacity and limited company exposure to cross-contamination potential at third-party sites.

Business Specialist-Site Operations (1996-1998)
Completed in six months and on schedule, a project that established all services for new, 1.3 million-square-foot complex on 325 acres, ensuring smooth transition to new facilities.
- Supervised more than 80 people in delivering all services to three companies at new site.
- Developed procedures for working with managed services with an annual budget of $2.5 million.
- Worked with contractors to set performance standards, monitor performance, suggest improvements, and ensure compliance.

EDUCATION

M.B.A., Ohio State University (2000)
B.S. in Business Management, Bowling Green University, OH (1996)

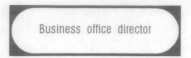
Business office director

OMKAR KHETTRY

921 Willow Lane
Mawtucket, CT 06323

(203) 555-7882
Khettry@access.net

PROFILE
- MBA in Finance, HFMA Fellow (FHFMA) and Certified Manager of Patient Accounts.
- Five years experience as hospital business office director.
- Knowledgeable and skilled in working with hospital department managers, physicians, and administration to improve bottom line.
- Strong customer and patient relation skills.

WORK EXPERIENCE

Business Office Director, Milton Memorial Hospital, Mawtucket, CT (1998-present)

Manage accounts receivable, insurance, collections, inpatient, outpatient and emergency room registrations, switchboard, and all telephone system administration for 250-bed facility. Provide budgeting and cost-reports assistance. Supervise and schedule up to 40 employees.

- Recommended new computer software, which provides more detailed patient information and allows hospital administrators to evaluate the need for current and future services.
- Established new collections policy, which increased collection of unpaid bills by 70 percent.
- Initiated new follow-up process with insurance companies, which has enhanced relations with carriers and patients and resulted in more timely payments to hospital.
- Honored for bringing office to highest production level ever in just two years.

Graduate Assistant, University of Connecticut School of Business, Danbury (1996-1998)

Provided class instruction for undergraduate students, including evaluating student projects and assigning final grades. Conducted research for professors.

- Assisted with School of Business career counseling program, which provided students with guidance in job searching, resume writing, and job interviewing.
- Formed committee that reviewed and revised current undergraduate and graduate requirements to better prepare students for the job market.
- Named 1998 "Outstanding MBA Student" for contributions to MBA program.

EDUCATION

MBA in Finance, Cum Laude, University of Connecticut, Danbury, 1998
BS in Marketing, Magna Cum Laude, University of Connecticut, Danbury, 1996

PROFESSIONAL ORGANIZATIONS

Chairman, Healthcare Policy Committee, Eastern Chapter, Healthcare Financial Management Association, Danbury, CT (2000-present)
Board Member, Northeast Region, National Guild of Patient Account Managers (2001-present)

RONALD G. LAMB

9575 N. 450 E.
Bismarck, ND 58501

(701) 555-1022
Cell: (701) 555-9754

Objective

A carpenter position with a residential builder that provides the opportunity to further develop trim-carpentry and electrical-wiring skills.

Skills Profile

- Two years experience in residential construction and framework.
- Ability to accurately interpret blueprints.
- Good background in residential wiring, trim carpentry, and crew management.
- Experienced in general construction and facility maintenance.

Work Experience
2001-present

Carpenter Framer and Roofing Crew Manager, Scott Construction, Bismarck, ND
Serve as carpenter framer for residential builder. Construct one-family homes, decks and porches and complete roofing projects on existing homes.

- Manage roofing crew of three, which has completed all assigned residential roofing projects on schedule and on budget.
- Designed 400-square-foot home deck and successfully managed construction crew of two.
- Have assisted in trim carpentry on three $250,000+ homes, including crown molding and mantle work.
- Have assisted in two residential wiring projects under supervision of licensed electrician.

1999-2001

General Laborer, Neese Farms, Inc., Bismarck, ND
Provided general maintenance on farm equipment, out buildings, and livestock and grain facilities. Mixed feed and cared for 300-head cattle herd.

- Assisted farm owner in completely re-wiring 100-year-old, two-story house, including removing copper fittings and adding 25 outlets and four ground faults.
- Helped construct 2,500-square-foot pole barn and shop area; set frames and supervised pouring of concrete floor and foundation.

1995-1998
(Summers)

Sales Clerk, Mace Hardware, Bismarck, ND
Handled stocking and helped manage inventory. Completed register sales.

- Recommended new display that better grouped supplies and idea/suggestion sheets for common home projects, saving customers time and extra trips for overlooked supplies; new displays received high customer satisfaction ratings.

Education

Indian Trails High School, Bismarck, ND (1999)

Activities

Making solid oak furniture and scroll-saw silhouettes

ELISABETH GARCIA
932 S. Woodrow Lane
Atlanta, GA 30128
www.EGarcia.net/home
Cell phone: (404) 555-9211

SUMMARY OF QUALIFICATIONS

- Licensed professional engineer with nearly 10 years experience completing multi-million dollar construction projects.
- Able to monitor, update, and successfully meet construction schedules and finish at or under budget.
- Capable of sequencing work to maintain existing operations.
- Skilled in project budgeting and cost analysis with excellent background in estimating.
- Experienced in bidding and contracting construction work.

PROFESSIONAL EXPERIENCE

Williams Mathau, Inc., Atlanta, GA

Project Manager (1999-present)
- Managed construction of a $135M, 520,000-square-foot research facility for a major pharmaceuticals firm.
- Developed and implemented new bidding procedure that resulted in 15% more contracts.
- Successfully bid/contracted more than $90M of work.
- Serve as trainer for in-house seminars on time management and procedures.

Project Manager (1998-1999)
- Managed construction of a $20M, 1,500-space parking structure for major research firm.
- Performed cost/design analysis of post-tension CIP and precast microsilica structural frames.
- Supervised engineering team of 15.

Assistant Project Manager (1997-1998)
- Managed construction of $5.5 million underground pedestrian connector for major research center.
- Successfully sequenced work across major roadway, resulting in uninterrupted traffic flow and minimal construction congestion.
- Initiated project procedures for contractors and staff, which reduced submittals and enhanced completion of project time line.

**PROFESSIONAL
EXPERIENCE**

Miles & McGill Co., Houston, TX

Project Engineer (1995-1997)
- Served as engineer on $16M, 85,000-square-foot concourse and $18M, 1,500-space parking structure for Houston Airport Authority.
- Handled all project schedule monitoring/updating.
- Expedited submittals and materials to complete project ahead of schedule.

Project Engineer (1994-1995)
- Served as project engineer on $2.5M utility relocation program for major research facility.
- Relocated chilled water mains, purified water, and high voltage electrical feeds.
- Sequenced work to maintain existing plant operations, allowing plant staff to complete projects on schedule and meet customer needs, unaffected by construction progress.

Assistant Project Engineer (1993)
- Served as assistant engineer on a $15M, 100,000-square-foot printing press facility.
- Handled weekly schedule monitoring/updating.
- Expedited fabrication and delivery of materials to ensure timely project completion.

Scheduling and Estimating Training, Manager of Scheduling (1991-1993)
- Performed quantity take-offs and data base estimating.
- Promoted to Manager of Scheduling after one year.

**EDUCATION/
LICENSING**

Licensed Professional Engineer in the State of Georgia (1998)
Masters of Science Degree in Civil Engineering, Texas A&M (1992)
Bachelor of Science Degree in Construction Management
  Engineering, Purdue University, West Lafayette, IN (1991)

MEMBERSHIPS

District Officer, Georgia Chapter of ASCE (1999-present)
Chairman, St. Joseph's Church Building Committee (1998-present)
- Managed $.5M building expansion, finishing it on schedule and on budget.

Brian Holloway
336 N. Salem Ave.
Cincinnati, OH 45205
(513) 555-8282

PROFILE

Extensive background in grain merchandising and commodity exporting on inland waterways and truck lines. Skilled in expanding business by developing new customers and services. Adept at contract negotiation and managing risk aspects for commodities. Experienced in export bagging operations and direct transfer business.

CAREER HISTORY

Director, Haverford Barge Company, Cincinnati, OH   **1999-present**
Responsible for profit/loss for $1.5M export facility. Provide general terminal services sales for 12 Midwest river facilities.

- Manage daily merchandising and personnel for Ohio export facility, which has achieved gross sales of more than $40M in last two years, a 45% increase.
- Oversee labor supply and services contract from third party.
- Negotiate all purchases and sales contracts with exporters.
- Expanded business by developing new European customers in Spain, France, and Portugal.
- Quantify and manage all risk aspects for commodities and negotiate all freight and FOB arrangements.
- Represent and sell transfer services to various large customers that use one or more transfer points.
- Package rail, barge, and transfer rates for river loading/unloading stations.

Sales/Special Projects Manager, Haverford Barge Company, Cincinnati, OH   **1996-1999**
Coordinated all sales work for products other than whole grain at largest river facility.

- Handled all customer contracts and sales for 750,000-ton fertilizer warehouse, export bagging operation, and more than 500,000 tons of direct transfer business received on an annual basis.
- Completed contracts with ocean freight companies for bagging contracts and took program to more than 40,000 short tons in the first year.
- Developed and directed small fleet of owners/operators to expand business and take advantage of various seasonal trucking opportunities.
- Negotiated and implemented a contract with a major firm to stevedore all capital equipment installed in a new auto manufacturing plant at Evansville, Ind.

CAREER HISTORY (cont.)

Grain Merchandiser/Special Projects Manager, Inland Transport, St. Louis, MO **1994-1996**
Director, Inland Truck Line, St. Louis, MO
One of two merchandisers responsible for originating grain on an FOB truck basis in four Plains states. Became director of Inland Truck Line in 1995.

- Completed daily balancing of all position and hedging activity.
- Supervised five employees on second-shift barge loading crew.
- Expanded services by establishing truck line and acquiring necessary regulatory approval to transport various commodities, including steel, scrap, ore, and coal.
- Grew operation from one to three full-time employees.
- Exceeded all first-year forecasts by netting $170,000.

Grain Merchandiser, Inland Transport, St. Louis, MO **1991-1994**
One of three merchandisers responsible for originating grain from farmers and elevators in three Midwest states.

- Maintained daily position balancing reports, month-end accounting, and projections.
- Recommended and implemented procedures for delayed pricing positions and spread positions, which were incorporated at all company facilities.
- Helped establish and assisted in daily operation of new subsidiary, which transported general commodities throughout the 48 contiguous United States.

EDUCATION

B.S., Agricultural Economics, University of Illinois, Champaign/Urbana (1991)

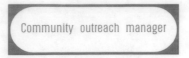

JANET W. ENGLISH

4460 Parker Road
Livonia, Michigan 48152

(313) 555-3553
JWEng@mailuser.net

SUMMARY OF SKILLS

Registered nurse with solid background in health education and social work. Skilled in developing programs and services that directly address community needs and achieve desired results. Experienced in working with community leaders and government agencies to successfully implement programs.

WORK EXPERIENCE

1996-present

St. Elizabeth Hospital, Detroit, Mich.

Community Outreach Manager (2001-present)
Manage neighborhood office, which provides educational services and works to improve living conditions for 2,000 of city's poorest citizens in run-down housing project. Secure grants to fund services and programs. Coordinate work with variety of community and government agencies. Supervise two-member staff.

- Established Resident's Council and led community survey, which determined resident's needs and goals.
- Worked with council and other agencies, including Housing and Urban Development (HUD), to secure grants and build affordable housing for area residents, with June 2003 projected completion date.
- Create and direct family and youth programs, which have reduced area vandalism and juvenile crime.
- Plan and supervise variety of educational and job-training programs, which provide residents with needed information and skills.
- Currently working on program to reduce infant mortality rate by establishing neighborhood store where mothers may "purchase" maternity and baby items with coupons received for obtaining pre-natal and well-baby care.

WORK EXPERIENCE

Community Outreach Coordinator (1999-2001)

Managed outreach program that works with community leaders and residents to care for emotionally, spiritually, medically, and financially needy residents. Managed budget and two staff members.

- Supervised survey to determine needs of rural community and developed necessary resources and staff to address identified issues.
- Worked with community to establish co-operative daycare, which provides quality childcare and helps adults develop job skills and learn good parenting skills.
- Developed mobile health program, staffed by hospital medical residents, to provide pre-natal and well-baby care.
- Created referral system with cooperation from local ministerial board, school system, physicians, and county offices, which helps residents secure needed services.
- Initiated and implemented hearing and health screenings in local festivals and fairs that target the elderly and determine their health care needs.

GYN/Oncology RN (1996-1999)

Cared for routine GYN post-surgery patients and GYN oncology patients. Administered chemotherapy and cared for routine post-partum and C-section patients.

- Earned 1998 Quality Care Award.

EDUCATION

1996   B.S. in Nursing, University of Michigan, Ann Arbor

ACTIVITIES

Volunteer Educator, Campaign for Healthy Babies, Detroit

Jeanne D. Temple

905 Edgewood Dr.
Prairie, ID 70012

(902) 555-1044
TempleJ@hayoo.com

Summary of Qualifications

- ▸ Eight years experience in park and recreation management, including implementing creative programs to increase interest in the park and benefit the community.
- ▸ Solid background in facilities management and maintaining attractive park grounds.
- ▸ Skilled administrator with experience in fund raising and budget management.

Work Experience

Parks Director, Prairie Parks System, Prairie, ID (1997-present)

Manage two community parks and six employees. Chair board of directors and oversee $400,000 budget. Monitor and enhance ecological aspects of park.

- ▸ Initiated and implemented variety of new programs, such as photography contest, Easter egg hunt, summer community band concerts, Haunted Trail, hayrides, and annual volleyball tournament, which have increased participation in park activities.
- ▸ Secured funding and managed $125,000 building expansion, which provided new baseball park press box and improved protection for maintenance and playground equipment.
- ▸ Established "Trees to Remember" program, which allows residents to donate trees as memorials and enhances park's ecological balance.
- ▸ Worked with civic organizations and Boise Symphony Orchestra to establish "Symphony at Sunset at Prairie Park," which draws people to the park, provides cultural opportunity and enhances orchestra's visibility in rural area.

Assistant Parks Director, Glendale Park System, Glendale, ID (1994-1997)

Developed educational programs and supervised grounds-keeping and picnic shelters for four-park system.

- ▸ Supervised park swimming pool renovation, which finished one week ahead of schedule and $10,000 under budget.
- ▸ Worked with athletic trainer to develop park fitness walk, which provided educational material and suggested exercise programs for a variety of age and ability levels.
- ▸ Initiated and conducted summer camps, which included teaching school-age children about ecology and biology to increase their interest in the sciences.

Biology Teacher, Glendale Community School Corp., Glendale, ID (1992-1994)

Instructed junior high and high school students in biology and general science.

- ▸ Designed ecological learning center and outdoor lab, which provided students with opportunity to study relationships between living things and their environments.

Education/Licensing

Bachelor of Science in Biology, University of Idaho, Boise (1992)
  Minor: Horticulture
Idaho State Teaching License (1992)

Sara Gutierrez
23 Marsh Road • Woodbridge, New York • 10912 • (914) 555-2009 • SMGuterrez@mymail.net

Summary of Qualifications
Eight years of experience in programming, system development, and system administration. Extensive UNIX background. Comprehensive knowledge of personal computer software. hardware, and peripherals. Well-versed in delivering technical presentations. Outstanding analytical skills. Seasoned Internet user.

Programming languages
C/C++, Pascal, Empress 4GL, SQL, Embedded SQL, FORTRAN, Perl, BASIC

Platforms
IRIS workstation, MS DOS, MS Windows, Interactive 386 UNIX, Macintosh, VAX

Work Experience
Programmer/Analyst, New World Systems, Whitehall, NY (2000-present)
- Enhance and support a relational database application used by the U.S. Government.
- Handle software development, database administration, system administration, future requirements planning, PC hardware/software support, user support, and daily operations.
- Implemented major improvements in automation of administrative and operational procedures, including distributed-database updates and data integrity checks, data transmission processes, managerial status reports, and data backup, which allows programmers more time to work on upgrade and development tasks.
- Reduced client's operating and maintenance costs by porting code from mainframe to code on microcomputer systems.
- Worked with Interactive UNIX and a variety of other languages and platforms to complete project.

Programmer/Designer, Lincoln Research Center, Sun City, FL (1995-2000)
- Investigated new fuselage design techniques for advanced aircraft design using computational fluid dynamics and unstructured-mesh computer modeling of aircraft geometries.
- Conducted a space vehicle packaging study using specialized CAD software and computational hypersonic aerodynamic models.
- Worked as part of a research team studying turboprop configurations in a low-speed wind tunnel, which led to improved aircraft design and performance.
- Upgraded and corrected a sonic-boom prediction program, which provided more accurate measurements and information.

Education
B.S. in Aeronautics, Massachusetts Institute of Technology, 1995, *Cum Laude*

Linda T. Gillespie

901 S. Hemingway
Millwood, NY 10531

(914) 555-2232
www.gillespie02.com

**PROFESSIONAL
PROFILE**

Published software professional with expertise in automatic English analysis, including text critiquing, text abstracting, and multimedia retrieval. Strong background in applied research and linguistics. Excellent programming skills. Software patent pending.

**PROFESSIONAL
EXPERIENCE**

2001-present

Consultant, It's Academic Inc., New York City, NY
- Provide specialized consultation in automatic language analysis.
- Create programs for Microsoft Corporation, Educational Testing Service, and Columbia University.
- Developed an ambiguity resolution component for Microsoft, which selects appropriate senses for words that have multiple meanings.

1996-2001

Staff Programmer, Artificial Intelligence Department, FBP Corporation, Williams Research Center, Rochester, NY

Object-oriented Graphical Abstractor (1999-2001)
- Developed user interface issues related to displaying document abstracts graphically.
- Addressed issues of displaying and traversing graphical networks.

Multimedia Indexer (1998-1999)
- Enhanced retrieval of multi-media objects described by indexes.
- Developed dictionary relationships (synonym and taxonym), which expanded user queries to include related items.

Grammar and Style Checker (1996-1998)
- Served as member of critique team, which did pioneering work in writer's tools by developing the first tool based on a full syntactic parse.
- Handled user interface and performance issues including:
  - Incorporating suggested corrections into a text editor.
  - Supporting interactive changes to the text.
  - Enhancing servers to distribute CPU-intensive processing. across platforms and to handle multiple users.
  - Creating user profiles to allow users to specify personal preferences for style checking.

**PROFESSIONAL
EXPERIENCE**
1992-1996

**Senior Associate Programmer, Documentation Automaton Systems, FBP
Corporation, Federal Systems Division, Hopewell, VA**
- Developed documentation automation system to reduce production costs of documentation, resulting in $1.6M savings during the first four years.
- Negotiated an agreement for software to ensure compliance with U.S. military readability requirements, resulting in a $1.1 M savings.

LANGUAGES   C, Smalltalk, C++, PLl, REXX, Pascal, Windows, VM/CMS

**ENVIRONMENTS
EDUCATION**   MS in Computer Science, New York University, New York City (1999)
BS in Computer Science, The Ohio State University, Columbus (1992)

PUBLICATIONS   Gillespie, "Sense Disambiguation Using On-Line Dictionaries," *Natural Language Processing,* Academic Publishers, Inc., 2000.

Barker, Gillespie, and McFry, "Post-Recognizer Processing: Applications for Automatic Speech," *Signal Processing Conference,* 1998.

Gillespie and Knight, "Lexicons for Broad Coverage Semantics," *Lexical Acquisitions,* Davis Associates Publishers, 1997.

Davis and Gillespie, "The Experience of Developing a Large-Scale Natural Language Text Processing System," *Conference on Applied Natural Language Processing,* 1996.

PATENTS   Patent pending for "A Method for Indexing of Multimedia Objects"

AWARDS   Outstanding Technical Achievement Award, FBP Corporation (1996)
Outstanding Research Contributions Award, FBP Corporation (1999, 2000)

ACTIVITIES   Local Walk Coordinator, March of Dimes, Millwood, NY (1999-present)

THOMAS K. EDEN

32 S. Riverview
Ogden, Iowa 50113
(515) 555-7998
TKEden@powermail.com

Profile:
Award-winning writer and editor with extensive corporate communications background. Adept in developing and implementing communication plans and programs related to company consolidations. Good background in speech writing, media relations, and community events planning. Skilled in desktop publishing.

Experience:
1997 - present

Manager—Employee Communications, Nova TeleCommunications Co., Benton, Iowa (formerly General Telephone Co.)
Prepare, plan, and organize information communicated to company's 15,000 employees. Produce six publications designed to maintain and enhance employee morale, perception, and understanding of company missions.
- Initiated, researched, and developed comprehensive employee communications program redesign (including employee focus groups), which became the model for the new corporate headquarters.
- Developed and implemented communications plans for consolidating 17 operator service offices to 4 and 33 customer contact offices to 10.
- Revised publication production schedule and method to decrease publication costs by 30%.
- Recommended cost-cutting measures for annual executive conference, which reduced expenses by $17,000.

1995 - 1997

Administrator—External Communications, General Telephone Co., Benton, Iowa
Handled media relations and served as spokesperson for regional headquarters. Wrote all news releases and submitted headquarters-based news releases to state offices to be tailored for local use.
- Researched and wrote monthly bill insert covering customer, deregulation, and general-interest information.
- Established "hometown feature" program, releasing company newspaper articles to employee's local newspapers, enhancing the company's image in its communities.
- Reorganized monthly meeting schedule with state staffs to save department $4,500 monthly.
- Developed and implemented community relations/corporate-giving program, which donated more than $10,000 to local organizations based on employee involvement.

Experience:

1993 - 1995

Employee Communications Administrator, Waldrop Corporation, Iowa City, Iowa
Prepared, edited, and distributed information to 5,000 employees in three states. Developed strike communication plan.
- Wrote, organized and compiled "briefing book," including company, geographical, governmental, economic, and community information for use with visiting executives.
- Investigated and established electronic mail procedures, which enhanced timely communication to employees and basically eliminated paper and printing costs.
- Inherited struggling management publication and made it an award-winning piece.
- Managed informal communications program where executives met with groups of employees over breakfast; survey results revealed increased trust among employees of company executives.

1987 - 1993

Assistant Editor, *Daily Time,* **Flora, Iowa**
Began career as reporter for daily city newspaper, circulation 7,500. Promoted to city editor after three years and became assistant editor in November 1992.
- Implemented desktop publishing system and new printing equipment which significantly reduced production costs and increased production speed by 45%.
- Worked with advertising team to expand number of advertisers and develop special advertising promotions; increased advertising budget 30%.

Education:

Indiana University, Bloomington
Bachelor of Arts in Journalism (1986)

Achievements/Honors:

International Association of Business Communicators (IABC)
   Excellent Performance in Communication (EPIC) Award–
   First Place, Newspaper/Magazine (1999, 2000)
IABC EPIC Award–First Place, Employee Newsletter (1998, 2000)
IABC EPIC Award–First Place, Management Publication (1997)

JAMIE CALAHAN

1053 Alamo Way, Apt. 3B
Austin, TX 78788

(512) 555-9340
JCal@mycomp.net

Summary of Skills

Licensed cosmetologist with 12 years experience in styling, training, and management. Ability to successfully develop and implement special sales promotions. Strong customer service, purchasing, and inventory background.

Product Experience

Shampoos: Redken, Nexxus, Matrix, Paul Mitchell, Sebastian, Image, Malibu 2000, Clairol, Brocato
Perms: Redken, Matrix, Nexxus, Helen Curtis, Revlon, Zotos
Color: Redken, Matrix, Sebastian, Framesi, Sunglitz, Goldwell
Nails: OPI, Creative Nail, Solar Nail

Training Experience

Assistant Redken Deco Color Trainer (1990-1993)
Sunglitz Technical Trainer (1997-1998)
OPI Nail Trainer (1995-1997)
Helene Curtis Perm Specialist (1994-1996)

Work Experience

Manager, Cut-ups Hair Salon, Austin, TX (1998-present)
➤ Operate salon under corporate policies, hire and train employees, handle payroll, and manage purchasing and inventory.
➤ Handle and address customer service problems.
➤ Initiated money-back guarantee program for four local stores, which increased monthly sales by $2,000.

Senior Stylist/Nail Technician, Macey Company, Austin, TX (1994-1998)
➤ Handled purchasing, inventory, cutting, coloring, perming, and styling for major department store chain salon.
➤ Served as team training leader and trained all new stylists.
➤ Recommended and implemented special services and equipment for handicapped customers at local store; program won local acclaim, increased sales, and was implemented in other company salons throughout the state.

Stylist/Assistant Manager, Hair By Design, Gateway, TX (1990-1994)
➤ Began as stylist; promoted to assistant manager after one year.
➤ Handled product orders, customer service, inventory, and all cosmetology services.
➤ Created special Mother's Day gift certificate promotion, which resulted in 14 new permanent customers for private salon.

Licensing

Anthony's Cosmetology College, Austin, TX (1990, Licensed Cosmetologist)

REBECCA WILSON
45 Oak Drive ✖ Wells, OH ✖ 43334 ✖ (419) 555-2667 ✖ Rebwil@mailbox.net

Profile

Seasoned counselor and manager with training in—and insight into—human behavior, with special emphasis on addictive behavior and crisis intervention. Experienced in developing and directing counseling programs. Skilled in assessing patients and developing and administering treatment plans.

Professional Experience

2000 - present

Senior Outpatient Counselor, Center for Chemical Dependency, Memorial Hospital, Wells, OH
- Developed and implemented the center's first Domestic Violence Men's Group, enhancing the anger management and communication skills of abusers in a group setting.
- Updated and revised eating disorder program to include prevention education for family and friends of patient, resulting in fewer reported cases and increased awareness among those groups
- Provide group after-care counseling.
- Conduct individual counseling of dual disorder (chemical dependency and mental illness) clients.

1997 - 2001

Primary Case Manager, Bowen Counseling Center, Bedford, OH
- Served as Float Counselor in Intensive Psychiatric, Multi-Axis, and Geroaddiction units.
- Assessed clients and developed master treatment plans, objectives, and methods.
- Established guidelines for counselor discharge summaries to comply with insurance company requirements, resulting in faster claims results for patients and the center.
- Organized four continuing education workshops, including hiring educators, securing classroom facilities, arranging lunches, and providing necessary written materials.
- Developed and implemented sibling awareness and prevention program for families of teenage patients in Alcohol Unit; 95% of the graduates continued to be alcohol-free one year after completing program.

1993 - 1997

Chaplain, Bowen Counseling Center, Bedford, OH
- Assessed patients and developed master treatment plans, involving chaplaincy goals, objectives, and methods.
- Led weekly grief/loss workshops, spirituality groups, step groups, and individual and couples continuing care groups.
- Established and led support group for couples who had lost an infant at birth.
- Scheduled all chaplaincy events.

Volunteer Experience

1998 - present

Volunteer, Green County Caring Center, Wells, OH
- Provide emotional counseling for six of the Caring Center's needy clients.
- Refer all clients to appropriate county assistance agencies.

2000 - present

Leader, Marriage Enrichment Program, Bedford Lutheran Church, Bedford, OH
- Developed and currently lead community program housed by local church.
- Created all lessons and written materials for program, which addresses and meets a community need.

1992 - 1993

Chaplaincy Internship, Green County Memorial Hospital, Waldon, OH
- Completed educational process provided in cooperation with Christian Theological Seminary to experience all phases of the chaplain's role.

1991 - 1992

Volunteer, Ohio Women's Prison, Columbus, OH
- Participated in crafts and conversation programs to enhance women's opportunities for positive interaction and increased self-esteem.

Education

1997   Sacred Theology Masters in Pastoral Counseling, Christian Theological Seminary, Columbus, OH

1993   Master of Divinity, Christian Theological Seminary, Columbus, OH

1990   Bachelor of Science in Psychology, The Ohio State University, Columbus, OH

Certification/State Licensing

1997   Certified Alcoholism Counselor

1996   Certified Marriage and Family Therapist

Ordination

1993   Lutheran Church

Memberships   National Association of Pastoral Counselors
Ohio Association of Alcohol/Drug Abuse Counselors
Green County Council to Prevent Alcohol and Other Drug Abuse
Green County Task Force to Prevent Domestic Violence

Dance instructor

Victoria E. Marchetta • 19 Valley Drive • Cleveland, OH • 44101 • (216) 555-2334

Summary of Qualifications

More than 15 years in dance performance, instruction, and troupe management. Skilled in developing private dance programs and in managing professional dance theaters, including fund raising, promotions, and performance scheduling. Experienced in establishing and administering student scholarship programs and innovative exchange programs.

Professional Experience

Director, Victoria Machetta School of Dance, Cleveland, OH
1989-present

Develop and schedule classes, supervise 15 faculty and staff members, and manage advertising, public relations, special events coordination, and day-to-day-operations. Serve as principal instructor for ballet technique and pointe.

- Maintain state, regional, and national reputation for dance program and ability to place students in major dance studios and help students earn scholarships to dance institutions, such as the University of Cincinnati and Julliard.
- Have instructed and placed students with national and international dance companies, such as the Cleveland Ballet, the Dance Theatre of Harlem, the Boston Ballet, and the National Ballet of Canada.
- Sponsored and manage liaison program with Cleveland Ballet Theatre, providing instructional experience for young professionals and unique learning experiences for dance students.
- Founded and manage summer scholarship program for dance students.

Artistic Director, Cleveland Ballet Theatre, Cleveland, OH
1997-present

Manage 50 dancers and artistic staff, setting, and staging for ballets, tour coordination, programming, and special events.

- Work with development (fund raising), marketing and public relations departments to secure corporate sponsorships of special presentations, which has enhanced troupe's image and increased attendance at all performances.
- Established and secured funding for exchange program with Russian ballet troupe, resulting in once-in-a-lifetime learning experiences for theater members and international performances for theater patrons.

Director, Great Lakes Ballet Ensemble, Cleveland, OH
1994-1997

Managed 30-member company, including tour scheduling, promotions, and performance programming.

- Worked with development department to establish special events and fund raisers that recognized and encouraged contributions from individuals, civic and philanthropic organizations, and businesses.
- Increased contributions 60% in two years.

Professional Experience

Choreographer
1987-present
Created, arranged, and directed dances at a variety of locations, including:
- Victoria Marchetta School of Dance (1987-present)
- Cleveland Ballet Theatre (1997-present)
- Great Lakes Ballet Ensemble (1994-1997)
- Cleveland Symphony Orchestra (1992-1994)
- Cleveland Civic Ballet, Inc. (1987-1992)

Ballet Mistress, Cleveland Civic Ballet, Inc.
1987-1992
Taught company class of 50 dancers and set and rehearsed ballets.

Performing Experience
Great Lakes Ballet Ensemble (1994-1995)
Cleveland Civic Ballet (1989-1992)
East Lake (Ohio) Summer Theatre (1986-1987)
Ohio University (Athens) Music and Art Camp (Summers 1984-1985)

Education
Markova Dance Studio, New York City, NY (1986)
The Jazz Studio, New York City, NY (1985)
School of American Ballet, New York City, NY (1984-1985)
Morgan Dance Studio, Cuyahoga Falls, OH (1970-1983)
Courses in Performing Arts, University of New York, New York City (1983, 1985)
- 9 credits in dance, 6 credits in performing arts, 12 credits in general studies

Courses Studied
Ballet Technique - Elizabeth Anderson, John Curry, Alexander Dumeo,
 Nancy Hatfield, Talia Markova, Judy Simms, Michael Todd, Guy Charisse
Pointe - Talia Markova, Michael Todd
Pas de Deux - Alexander Dumeo, John Curry
Modern - Judy Simms, Nancy Hatfield
Jazz - Nancy Hatfield, Elizabeth Anderson
Tap - Elizabeth Anderson, Judy Simms
Character - Guy Charisse, Judy Simms
Dance Terminology - Elizabeth Anderson, Nancy Hatfield, Michael Todd

LAURA McINTYRE

1203 Bayview Lane	(207) 555-9443 (home)
Sandy Hook, ME 03992	(207) 555-1002 (work)

SUMMARY OF SKILLS

- Strong background in early childhood care.
- Skilled in designing and implementing developmentally appropriate activities.
- Able to create and initiate hands-on learning experiences.
- Capable of developing nursery school curriculum.

EXPERIENCE

2000-present

Day-care Attendant, The Wonder Years Day Care, Sandy Hook, ME
Provide daily care and attention for children ages 2 to 10. Provide safe transportation for school-age children to and from local elementary school.

- Organize field trips for up to 30 preschoolers to local service agencies, the library, and other "learning" centers, which introduce children to the world around them.
- Initiated use of puppets and water and sand tables for 2- to 3-year-olds, encouraging creative play and emphasizing hands-on learning.
- Initiated morning nursery school program for children not in daily daycare, which met a community need and enhanced the daycare center's total program.
- Assisted manager in creating and teaching nursery school curriculum and related activities for up to 15 children each week.
- Assisted manager in planning and establishing special summer programs.
- Assisted manager in converting from manual to computerized bookkeeping, which reduced bookkeeping time and produced more accurate accounting/tax reports.

Summers 1996-1999

Childcare Provider, Sandy Hook, ME

- Ensured fun and safe play environment for three children ages 18 months to 5 years.
- Prepared snacks and lunches and cleaned up afterward.
- Maintained schedule, including naps and outside play time.
- Completed light housekeeping duties, such as dishwashing and vacuuming.

EDUCATION

Present	Courses toward an Associate's Degree in Early Childhood Education, Warsaw Junior College, Warsaw, ME (12 credits, 3.6/4.0 GPA)
1999	Graduate, Sandy Hook High School, Sandy Hook, ME

SUSAN MEREDITH
902 Vince Street
Lafayette, MT 59049
(406) 555-9091
Meredith_74@alo.com

OBJECTIVE   Expanded Duties Dental Assistant in a private office or dental clinic.

SUMMARY OF
QUALIFICATIONS
- Perform expanded duties such as rubber dam placement, pit and fissure sealants, and Classes I, II, V amalgam restorations, and Classes III, IV, V resin composite restorations.
- Complete a variety of lab work, including custom trays, temporary crown, pouring and trimming models, trimming dies, plaster cast, and stone dies.
- Prepare tray set-ups and assist during procedures, including fillings and crown preps.
- Clean and maintain X-ray processors, sterilize instruments.
- Obtain and record patient information, including current treatment and conditions; code insurance forms.

PROFESSIONAL
EXPERIENCE
2001 - present	Expanded Duties Dental Assistant, Dr. William Howard, D.D.S., Dayton, MT
2000 - 2001	Dental Assistant, Eastern Montana University School of Dentistry, Dayton, MT
1998 - 2000	Chairside Dental Assistant, Dr. Robert Smith, D.D.S., Lafayette, MT
1998	Extern Program, Dr. Richard Spencer, D.D.S., Warren, MT

EDUCATION/
CERTIFICATION
1999	Graduate, Warren High School, Warren, MT
1997 - 1999	W. G. Wright Career Center, Dayton, MT

- Completed curriculum and certification in dental assisting and maintained an "A" average while completing junior and senior years of high school.

HONORS
- Selected as third in the state in dental-assisting skills in 1998.
- Member of Top Ten in dental-assisting skills in the state in 1999.

Christopher A. Galloway

404 E. Main St., Apt. 11B
Winslow, OK 74112

(918) 555-1221
Cell Phone: (918) 555-0077

SUMMARY OF SKILLS

- Experienced on-air radio personality with excellent background in creative and technical aspects of radio/sound production.
- Able to adapt to a variety of radio program formats.
- Skilled at developing community involvement programs.

EXPERIENCE

2001 - present

Disc Jockey, KKXY, Winslow, OK
Handle daily disc jockey responsibilities for 20,000-watt radio station. Deliver public service announcements. Write, produce, and provide voice-overs for local commercials. Assist in determining program format.

- Initiated community involvement program with local hospital to offer free health and hearing screenings, which addresses need for quality preventive health care in high-risk population.
- Established fund-raising events on radio air time to benefit Senior Citizens Center and Boys' and Girls' Club, generating nearly $2,000 annually for each group.
- Nominated for Outstanding New Radio Personality by Oklahoma Radio Association.

Owner, Galloway Sound Design, Winslow, OK
Provide sound design consultation and set-up for a variety of clients.

- Manage sound design for Winslow Community School Corporation, including student dances and musical and drama productions.

1999 - 2001

Disc Jockey/Assistant Station Manager, KCKC, Jacksonville Vocational Community College, OK
Implemented station policies and procedures. Supervised staff of two.

- Introduced new advertising promotion, which increased sales 30%.

EDUCATION

2001

Associate's Degree in Telecommunications, Jacksonville Vocational Community College, OK (3.7/4.0 GPA)

ACTIVITIES

Advisor/Guest Instructor, Vocational Radio/Television Course, Winslow Community School Corporation, Winslow, OK

NATHAN P. ZIMMERMAN
901 Market St.
Jackson, MS 39232
(601) 555-1992
Cell Phone: (601) 555-0947

SKILLS SUMMARY

More than 12 years experience in dispatch and driver management. Solid background in scheduling and coordinating delivery dates and times. Good customer-relations skills.

WORK EXPERIENCE

1996-present

Dispatcher, Holden Transit Company, Jackson, MS
Manage dispatching for up to 60 moving van and flatbed drivers.
- Solicit freight from freight brokers, and contact trip lease and port agents to secure flatbed loads.
- Order and procure permits and escorts for over-dimensional, interstate flatbed loads.
- Develop and quote transportation rates to shippers and agents.
- Recommended and implemented new scheduling system, which reduces road hours for drivers and has improved driver safety record.

1989-1995

Medical Technician, United States Air Force, Honolulu, HI
Assisted in medical care of sick and injured military patients. Scheduled and trained personnel. Managed equipment, supplies, and inventory.
- Supervised Aero Medical Evacuation, including coordinating arrival and delivery dates and times of air evacuation missions with Army and Navy personnel.
- Oversaw conversion of cargo aircraft to air evacuation status, which provided needed medical aircraft while making good use of older aircraft.
- Supervised 20-bed surgical ward.

1988-1989

Customer Service Representative, Stevenson Lumber, Jackson, MS
Handled customer service requests and inquiries.
- Prepared and coordinated orders for delivery.
- Implemented computerized inventory and delivery system.

EDUCATION

Certificate of Management, Jackson Community College, MS (2000)

CERTIFICATION

Certified Emergency Medical Technician—State of Mississippi

ACTIVITIES

Volunteer, Meyers Memorial Hospital, Jackson, MS

GARY SANDERS
4506 N. Vernon St.
Tecumseh, WI 53225
(414) 555-9203
G_Sanders@mailstar.net

Profile: Professional engineer with more than 15 years of experience in rural and municipal electric operations. Excellent supervision and labor relations. Ability to design and successfully implement cost saving and service-improving procedures. Skilled in system planning, preventive maintenance, budget management, and designing standardized procedures and training programs.

Work Experience:
1997-present

Engineering Manager, Madison County Rural Electric, Tecumseh, WI
Handle system planning, design, metering, substation maintenance, and provide technical consultation. Supervise four employees. Direct day-to-day, annual, and long-term engineering and planning.
- Coordinated program that reduced maintenance overtime, enhanced system reliability during major system disruptions, and reduced outage times for all nine substations.
- Managed peak-controlling equipment installation and start-up, which resulted in annual savings of nearly $200,000.
- Designed, developed, constructed, and installed voltage-control equipment for six substations for a total installed cost of under $1,000 each.
- Produced work plans for REA approval and budgetary purposes and directed return to standard REA construction specifications for all construction projects.
- Produced the first set of company-wide job descriptions with associated organizational chart.
- Handled economic evaluation of various projects, such as diesel engines for trucks and low-loss transformers.

1994-1997

Assistant Manager, Albion Power II: Light, Albion, WI
Supervised three departments and 45 employees for 6,000-meter company with $3.5 million annual sales.
- Assisted manager in reducing nearly $500,000 power bill indebtedness to 2 percent positive margin in two years.
- Closed out-of-date, high-cost generation station while increasing financial margins and maintaining full employment for all 40 employees.
- Assisted manager in reorganizing operation, including new job descriptions and responsibilities for power plant, distribution, and office personnel in a union environment.

Work Experience:

1991-1994   **Assistant Manager, Albion Power & Light, Albion, WI**
Organized preventive maintenance program. Researched programs for future power supplies.
➤ Designed and implemented various standardized procedures and training programs, which reduced procedural errors.
➤ Oversaw clerical help handling billing, cash receipts, accounts receivable and payable, auditing, and general record keeping.
➤ Initiated and completed change over to computerized billing system, which reduced a three-month backlog.

1987-1991   **Staff Engineer, Morrow and Company, Walters, WI**
Coordinated and managed major repair and maintenance projects up to $750,000.
➤ Designed and implemented preventive maintenance program for major power substation and distribution facilities.
➤ Recommended and designed new training program, which reduced procedural errors.

1985-1987   **Substation Designer, Cooperative Education Student, Public Service Wisconsin, Madison, WI**
➤ Completed design projects as assigned by staff engineer.
➤ Assisted in standardizing training manuals and enhancing engineering operations.
➤ Gained experience supervising and working with union employees.

Education:

1987   B.S. in Electrical Engineering Technology, *with honors*
Wisconsin State University

Memberships:

1989-present   American Association of Electrical Engineers
1997-present   Advisor, Wisconsin State University Association of Student Engineers

Related Activities:

2000-present   Project Leader, 4-H Electronics Project, Madison County 4-H, Tecumseh, WI

ANNA WHITE CLOUD

(After Dec. 15, 2002)
154 Columbia St.
Sierra, NM 87002
(505) 555-4667
Whitecloud@quick.net

(Until Dec. 15, 2002)
519 University St., #3B
Albuquerque, NM 87112
(505) 555-1992
Whitecloud@quick.net

SKILLS SUMMARY

Solid background in environmental and wildlife education. Skilled in working with the public and increasing understanding of ecological issues. Experienced in maintaining park facilities and trails. Fluent in Spanish.

EXPERIENCE

2001-present

Recreation Management Intern
High Sierra Forest Preserve, NM
Provide visitors with information on ecology, environmental resources, and forest management. Lead guided tours and informative discussions on environmental issues.

- Developed and present educational program on wildlife habitats.
- Created new walking trail, which provides visitors with guided tour to tracking wildlife.

1998-2001

Volunteer/Summer Intern
Apache National Forest, NM
Met visitors at Visitor's Center, answered questions and provided trail maps. Assisted forest rangers in inspecting and maintaining public facilities, shelters, trail markers, and monuments.

- Helped develop new educational program on wildlife management for Visitor's Center.
- Designed new trail map, which coordinated with color-coded trail markers and explained degrees of hiking difficulty.

EDUCATION

Bachelor of Science in Recreation Management, University of New Mexico, Albuquerque (Expected Dec. 2002)
Related course work: environmental resources, biology, ecology, park management, recreational resource planning, and public relations.

ACTIVITIES

Volunteer, Museum of Native American Culture, Albuquerque, NM

Carol A. Lafferty • 1442 W. Wilshire Ct. • Oklahoma City, OK • 73102 • (405) 555-9822

Summary of Qualifications

Skilled administrator with nearly 10 years experience in executive administration, marketing, and sales management, including program and trade show coordination. Solid background in office computer operations, office administration and training.

Professional Experience

Wellington Commercial Air Filters, Oklahoma City, OK

Executive Administrator, North American Products Group (2001-present)

Provide administrative and advisory support for corporate president and all international/regional vice presidents.

- Coordinate and implement international corporate projects, policies, procedures, ventures, and acquisitions.
- Implemented standardized office computer operations and software for domestic operations, with international implementation set for June 2004.

Executive Assistant, Automotive & Consumer Group (1999-2001)

Handled administrative and advisory support for corporate president.
Coordinated progress reporting and assignments of vice presidents. Planned and coordinated arrangements for all corporate meetings.

- Developed orientation and training program for administrative secretaries, which increased efficiency and productivity and reduced overlapping duties.
- Managed marketing and promotion of automotive racing program, which produced high name recognition for corporation domestically and abroad.

Marketing Assistant, Automotive & Consumer Group (1996-1999)

Served as corporate assistant to consumer and automotive marketing vice presidents, national sales managers, and senior product managers. Provided marketing support to 200-member sales force. Assisted in promoting automotive racing program.

- Compiled and analyzed sales/marketing reports, oversaw new product implementation, and supervised customer inquiries.
- Implemented new competitive analysis procedure, which helped establish short- and long-term corporate marketing goals.

Marketing Professionals International, Tulsa, OK

Program Administrator-Affiliate Services (1993-1996)

Provided administrative support management for 15,000-member trade organization. Supervised all programs undertaken by 100 affiliated organizations. Handled public speaking, membership development, convention and program planning, trade show coordination, and printing and advertising for all marketing promotions.

- Increased membership 25% in two years.

Education

Bachelor of Science in Business Administration, Tulsa State College, Tulsa, OK (1993)

- Concentration in Administrative Management

JEFFREY D. FOUNDARY
703 Meadow View Rd., #24
Charleston, WV 25339
(304) 555-2992
Jeffdf@mail.net

SUMMARY OF QUALIFICATIONS

Exercise scientist with excellent experience in prescribing and supervising exercise programs, performing therapeutic modalities, and conducting clinical exercise and health-screening tests. Skilled in developing educational and training materials.

CLINICAL SKILLS/ABILITIES

➤ Perform rehabilitative modalities, including ultrasound, electrical stimulation, whirlpool, iontophoresis, paraffin, and TENS unit.
➤ Conduct work conditioning with BTE Work Simulator and LIDO Weight Machine.
➤ Assess resting metabolic rate (Beckman Horizon Metabolic Cart) and resting electrocardiogram (Quinton ECG Cart).
➤ Test pulmonary functions with Puritan-Bennett, Gould Spirometer, and Respirodyne II.
➤ Test strength with Kin-Com III Isokinetic Dynamometer.
➤ Assess body composition, including hydrostatic weighing with nitrogen analysis, Valhalla Medical 1990B Bio-Impedance, and skinfold calipers.

PROFESSIONAL EXPERIENCE

Physical Abilities Testing Coordinator/Exercise Specialist, Methodist Hospital Industrial Rehabilitation Center, Charleston, WV (2001-present)

Implemented and market Physical Abilities Testing (PAT) Program. Organize and administer on-site job analysis, conduct physical abilities tests. and administer PAT certification training sessions. Develop all necessary educational materials.

➤ Supervise work conditioning sessions, including orientation and instruction.
➤ Assist occupational therapist in hand clinic with rehabilitative therapy for acute and chronic injuries.
➤ Maintain and order equipment and therapy supplies.

Health Screening Specialist, Occupational Health Consulting Corporation, Charleston, WV (1999-2001)

Administered on-site corporate health screenings, including health-risk assessment, flexibility and body composition. Organized staffing and scheduling for corporate health screenings.

➤ Developed and implemented screening protocols and educational materials.
➤ Initiated and developed staff training manual and training program.
➤ Conducted individual consultations with clients immediately following screenings.

PROFESSIONAL EXPERIENCE

Exercise Specialist, The Fitness Center, Charleston, WV (1998-1999)

Administered exercise tests and fitness screenings, including graded exercise tests, muscular strength and endurance.

➤ Developed exercise prescriptions for clients.
➤ Recommended and created fitness screening manual, protocols, and results handout, which provided necessary educational and follow-up information.

Exercise Specialist Intern, Center for Health and Fitness Services, Charleston, WV (1998)

Administered maximal and sub-maximal exercise tests and fitness assessments. Developed exercise prescriptions and assisted with on-site health screenings.

➤ Presented fitness seminars to community groups, which helped educate the public about proper fitness and training.
➤ Participated in research project on exercise in older adults.

Student Athletic Trainer, West Virginia University, Wheeling, WV (1995-1998)

Performed treatment, preventive, and rehabilitative techniques for acute and chronic athletic injuries.

➤ Served as physical therapy aid in University Hospital.

EDUCATION

B.S., Exercise Science/Counseling Psychology, West Virginia University, Wheeling (1998)

CERTIFICATIONS

➤ Certified CPR Rescuer/Community First Aid and Safety, American Red Cross
➤ Certified Ergonomic Specialist, Ergonomics, Inc.

AFFILIATIONS

➤ Member, American College of Sports Medicine

ACTIVITIES

➤ Weightlifting
➤ Marathon running

KENT L. McCARTHY
19 E. Walnut St.
Atlanta, GA 31113

(404) 555-3343   Cell Phone: (404) 555-7054

PROFILE

Skilled manager with more than 10 years experience in defining and achieving organizational performance goals. Able to strategically plan direction of rapidly evolving public safety agency. Adept at designing and implementing innovative management policies, processes, and programs.

CAREER HISTORY

1992-present

Fire Chief, Chief Executive Officer
Center County Fire Department, Atlanta, Ga.
Develop, administer, and manage multi-faceted municipal fire department currently employing 160 full-time personnel and serving one of state's rapidly growing, most populous counties. Establish mission and long-range goals, plan objectives and policies, organize human and material resources, direct subordinate chief officers, staff personnel and division managers, and manage $10M annual budget.

- Managed department's transition from volunteer fire department to current status as one of state's 10 largest fire departments.
- Designed and implemented an integrated, state-of-the-art management system with structured and well-defined policies, procedures and processes for recruit selection, performance appraisal, promotion, discipline, and more.
- Established system of standard operating procedures that directs and controls all facets of department's emergency operations; one of first in state to successfully implement nationally recognized Incident Command System.
- Designed and implemented Career Development Plan, which provides employees with opportunity to attain career-advancement skills.
- Established one of state's first mandatory physical fitness programs, which has decreased frequency of work-related injuries and increased employees' stamina in hostile environments.

1997-present

Subcommittee Chairman
Atlanta Hazardous Materials Emergency Planning Committee, Ga.
Chair subcommittee charged with designing and implementing a task force to respond to emergency incidents involving hazardous materials.

- Coordinate and secure commitment from fire, law enforcement, EMS and other public and private sector agencies in three-county area.
- Introduced local ordinances and state legislation regarding emergency plans.

CAREER HISTORY
1985-1992   **Firefighter/EMT, Paramedic, Company Officer**
Fulton County Fire Department, Atlanta, Ga.
- Initiated department's advanced life support program and functioned as liaison officer between department and sponsoring hospital.
- Developed and implemented county's Rescue Diver Training program, which was the first in the tri-county area.
- First to be promoted to company officer after just three years of service.

EDUCATION

National Fire Academy, Emmitsburg, Md. (1995-1998)
- Executive Fire Officer Program

Georgia State University, Atlanta (1984-1985)
- 15 credit hours in management

AWARDS

Community Appreciation for Service in Public Enlightenment and Relations Award, Community Service Council of Northern Georgia (1997)
Community Service Award, Children's Bureau of Atlanta (1999)

PROFESSIONAL

Master Firefighter - Fire Prevention

CERTIFICATIONS

Master Firefighter - Tactics
Master Firefighter - Fire Service Management
Master Firefighter - Instructor 1st Class
Master Firefighter - Aircraft Crash and Rescue
Firefighter - First Class
State of Georgia - Emergency Paramedic
State of Georgia - Emergency Medical Technician - Primary Instructor

PROFESSIONAL
AFFILIATIONS

International Association of Fire Chiefs
National Fire Protection Association
Georgia Fire Chiefs Association

COMMUNITY
ACTIVITIES

Chairman, Aluminum Cans for Burned Children Foundation, Atlanta
Planning Committee, Tri-County Home Safety Program for Children
Volunteer, Burn Unit, Atlanta General Hospital

WENDY BARTHOLOMEW

15 Northside Dr.
Brighton, LA 71134

(318) 555-2556
Wendy_DB@access.net

SUMMARY OF QUALIFICATIONS

- Experienced institutional food services manager with excellent background in menu planning, food preparation, and dietary consultation.
- Skilled in creating nutritious meals within a budget.
- Experienced in supervising union employees, purchasing, and forecasting.

PROFESSIONAL EXPERIENCE

1999-present

Food Service Director, MTE Corp., Martin Financial Services, Inc., Carthage, LA

- Supervise 20 employees providing service at corporate cafeteria.
- Worked with corporate secretarial staff to develop catering specifications for employee banquets previously held off-site; corporation accepted bid, bringing in an additional $30,000 per year.
- Created and introduced low-fat entree line, which increased sales $3,000 per month.

1996-1999

Food Service Manager, MTE Corp., Brighton Community School Corp., Brighton, LA

- Supervised 30 employees at six school sites.
- Handled personnel responsibilities, including hiring, dismissal, training, and payroll.
- Managed a $620,000 sales and $420,000 expense budget.
- Interacted with people at all levels of the organization, including students, teachers, school board members, and the administration.
- Initiated new purchasing procedure on computer system, resulting in more accurate forecasting.

1994-1996

Caterer, Marriott Educational Services, Southern University, Baton Rouge, LA

- Supervised and trained eight employees in food service.
- Served as maitre d' at university president's home.

1991-1992

Sales Clerk, Michael's Sportswear, Baton Rouge, LA

- Assisted customers in selecting clothing.
- Helped design and arrange window displays.
- Created "Mardi Gras" sales promotion, which increased sales 35% during promotion period.

EDUCATION

1994

Bachelor of Science Degree in Supervision/Associate Degree in Applied Science in Restaurant, Hotel and Institutional Management, Southern University, Baton Rouge, LA (3.8/4.0)

Graphic artist/video producer

TIM G. COLEMAN

821 Jackson St., Apt. 21B
Philadelphia, PA 19021

(215) 555-0220
TimCole@mailuser.net

SUMMARY OF SKILLS

Award-winning graphic artist with extensive experience in state-of-the-art technologies. Skilled in creating and successfully implementing new product lines to compete with market leaders. Also skilled in video production and computer-generated images, including creating two- and three-dimensional programs and commercials.

PROGRAMS AND SYSTEMS

- Macintosh and IBM systems
- CorelDraw! and Aldus PageMaker on IBM
- Adobe Photoshop, Adobe Illustrator, Aldus Freehand, Adobe Premier, Macromind Director, Strata Vision 3-D, Strata Studio Pro on Macintosh
- Commadore Amiga 4000 computer system running with "Video Toaster"
- 3-D animation using Lightwave 3-D
- 2-D animation using Brilliance

WORK EXPERIENCE

2001-present **Video Graphic Artist, Showtime Productions, Titus, PA**
- Create and edit short animation sequences for use in commercial and private video production.
- Alter still video pictures for use in broadcast video.
- Complete linear editing for a variety of projects.
- Researched and implemented use of Adobe Premier, which provides client with a non-linear hard copy of a planned commercial before investing in expensive production time, resulting in substantial savings for the client and the company.
- Created and produced 15 commercials and five short animation sequences in one year on part-time basis.

WORK EXPERIENCE

2000-present **Graphic Artist, National Card Co., Philadelphia, PA**
- Create designs and lettering for greeting cards, gift wraps, gift boxes, party goods and accessories using Adobe Illustrator, Aldus Freehand, Quark XPress, and Adobe Photoshop.
- Coordinate production of all items.
- Designed new children's humorous greeting card and gift wrap line, which increased sales in that area by 45%.
- Recommended and worked with sales representatives to introduce new line of coordinated party items, which successfully competes with current market leader.
- Created and currently coordinating production of new holiday gift wrap design.

1998-2000 **Graphic Artist, Creative Graphics, Willow, PA**
- Completed design work for a free-lance design group specializing in concept, layout, and production of original logos and identity systems.
- Completed 30 projects and assisted with 12 others.
- Created and implemented print advertising campaign, which expanded client base 25% and brought in three new major customers.

1998 **Design Artist, Margaret Sloan Gallery, Titus University, PA**
- Created a series of posters and postcards promoting professional and student work in the University galleries.
- Work was featured in a 1999 promotional brochure for the university.

EDUCATION

1998 Bachelor's Degree in Fine Arts, *Magna Cum Laude,* Titus University, PA
Minors: Computer Imaging, Drawing

AWARDS

2001 National Award Winner, American Paper Box Association
Silver award in folding carton design
Bronze award in ridged box design
2000 Finalist, National Print Magazine Cover Design Competition
1997 Accepted, Titus University Scholarship Show
1997 Scholarship Award for Outstanding Portfolio, National Card Co.

NATALIE W. SANDBERG • 5561 Walnut Dr. • Providence, RI 02811 • (401) 555-0992

SKILLS SUMMARY Champion gymnast with five years instructional experience. Adept at assessing students' skills and abilities and developing innovative, age-appropriate curriculum. Solid background in nutritional education.

WORK EXPERIENCE

2000-present **Gymnastics Instructor, The Dance Studio, Providence, RI**
Develop and teach gymnastics curriculum for preschool students (ages 1-5) at three class levels. Incorporate academic aspect into lessons by using colors, shapes, letters, and numbers. Train substitute instructors.
- Established "Moms and Tots" program, which has grown from one class to three classes per week.
- Created "theme" lessons, such as fire safety, the Big Top, and football season, which have been adopted by the National Gymnastics Association.
- Organize annual recital, which displays students' progress over the year.
- Coordinated special promotion, which increased number of students 20%.

1998-2000 **Gymnastics Coach, Campbell YMCA, Providence, RI**
Instructed 45 students, ages 6 to 12. Organized by age and ability into three class levels. Developed and monitored daily workouts and individualized weight training programs.
- Initiated nutritional education through weekly discussions and "mock" training table sessions.
- Coordinated competitive meets, including hiring judges, setting up and inspecting equipment, and securing event runners and awards.
- Placed six students in advanced summer training camps.

1997-1998 **Physical Education Teacher/Girls' Volleyball Coach, Walnut Grove High School, Walnut Grove, RI**
Developed daily lesson plans and organized classes to help students progress in their physical skills and knowledge of rules for a variety of sports and activities.
- Designed and developed skills tests and written tests for grade levels 9 through 12.
- Coached girls' volleyball team to regional championship.

1996-1997 (School year) **Gymnastics Instructor, Rhode Island State College, Providence**
Taught gymnastics classes offered by college for preschool through high school students. Helped develop preschool curriculum.

EDUCATION/ LICENSING B.S. in Physical Education, Rhode Island State College, Providence (1997)
Rhode Island State Teaching License (1997)

GYMNASTICS ACHIEVEMENTS Women's Gymnastics Team, Rhode Island State College, Providence
- Mental Attitude Award (1995-1997)
- Member, National Qualifying Team (1996)
State Champion, Walnut Grove High School Gymnastics Team (1992, 1993)

JUSTIN A. SHAFFER

56 N. Alamogordo Dr.
Phoenix, AZ 85002

(602) 555-4667
Justin27@hayoo.com

PROFILE

Skilled manager with five years experience in directing employee recruitment, training, and evaluation activities. Solid background in developing and implementing progressive and innovative evaluation and training programs to improve employee morale and reduce turnover.

EXPERIENCE

Human Resources Manager, Tuttle Enterprises, Phoenix, AZ (2000-present)

Manage employee recruiting, evaluation, and training programs and procedures for company with 1,500 employees. Review internal and external candidate applications and coordinate interviews with appropriate department and section heads.

- Established new performance evaluation and tracking procedure, which has increased employee satisfaction with review process 45%.
- Recommended and implemented automated, self-paced training program that provides employees with opportunity to acquire needed skills for advancement on company computers and company time.
- Reduced employee turnover 25% by June 2001.

Military Personnel Management/Programs Officer, Arizona Air National Guard, Midway Field, AZ (1999-2000)

Directed military personnel programs for Arizona Air National Guard (approximately 3,300 members). Established, implemented and managed personnel policies, incentive and promotion programs, and personnel utilization.

- Managed office automation systems and trained all personnel on computer use, software, and hardware.
- Increased office support capabilities and decreased required overtime by 50%.
- Became central coordinator for headquarters' enlisted members, including work assignments, training, awards, decoration, and promotion; innovative efforts led to documented positive impact on enlisted members' performance, production, and morale.

EDUCATION

B.S. in Business Administration, Arizona State University, Phoenix (1998)
Arizona Commendation Medal as Honor Graduate, Personnel Programs Officer Training, United States Air Force, Phoenix, AZ (1999)

GARY J. HENSLEY
51 S. Mayfield Dr. • Mobile, AL • 36607 • (205) 555-6003 • GJHensley@mymail.net

SKILLS SUMMARY   Nearly 20 years management experience in the insurance industry. Solid background in premium auditing, product management, underwriting and computer systems management. Skilled in developing and implementing training programs, online policy systems, and new products.

EMPLOYMENT HISTORY
1994-present

National Insurance Company, Mobile, AL
Premium Audit Manager (2001-present)
- Audit commercial book of business, including adjusting classifications and exposure.
- Communicate directly with independent agents to resolve audit disputes, which has enchanced working relationships between corporate office and field staff.
- Hire and train new staff on auditing guidelines and procedures.
- Supervise staff of five auditors and four support personnel.

Senior Staff Specialist, Product Management (2000-2001)
- Integrated Underwriting System into Product Management Department, which involved evaluating and placing personnel in appropriate positions.
- Maintained "common" screens for Commercial Automated System.

Underwriting Systems Manager (1997-2000)
- Developed, implemented, trained, and maintained corporate underwriting systems.
- Supervised staff of 30 with department budget in excess of $500,000.
- Provided training services to support automated and non-automated systems to 21 divisions and three service centers.
- Supervised automated rate files for 40 states, supporting more than 2 million policies and $1.5 billion in written premiums.

Comline Systems Manager (1994-1997)
- Developed first commercial online policy-issuing system for corporation.
- Implemented commercial online policy system in 15 divisions and three service centers.
- Developed training program and trained support personnel to maintain and enhance system.
- Supervised staff of 10.

EMPLOYMENT HISTORY

1982-1994

American Insurance Company Mobile, AL
Casualty Staff Specialist (1991-1994)
: Handled general liability, workers compensation and crime rates, rules, and forms for all operating states.
: Created "Ultra Contractors," a commercial product that currently has more than $70 million of premium in force.
: Developed manuals to support rates, rules, forms and underwriting systems.
: Supervised staff of six.

Commercial Policy Service Manager, East Divisions (1988-1991)
: Managed all commercial rating, statistical coding, and policy typing, representing more than $85 million premium dollars.
: Developed and implemented training program for commercial underwriting division.
: Supervised staff of 90.

Assistant Manager, Alabama Commercial Underwriting (1986-1988)
: Managed commercial underwriting and risk selection for approximately one-third of the state.
: Trained supporting underwriters, raters, and typists.
: Supervised staff of 15.

Senior Commercial Underwriter (1982-1986)
: Handled risk selections and underwriting for lines of general liability, workers compensation, commercial auto, crime, plate glass, and boiler and machinery.

EDUCATION

University of Alabama, Mobile
: 24 credit hours in General Studies (1981)

ACTIVITIES

Director, Mayfield Home Owners Association

Interior designer

LESLIE J. TODD

33 River Lane
Cincinnati, Ohio 45287

(513) 555-0922
LJT@powermail.com

SUMMARY OF SKILLS

More than 12 years in the interior design business, including specialized experience in restaurant and cafeteria planning and design. Skilled in developing elevations, floor plans, and reflected ceiling plans. Strong background in both commercial and residential projects.

WORK EXPERIENCE

2000-present

Owner/Designer, L. Todd Interiors, Cincinnati, Ohio
Own and operate interior design company serving residential and commercial customers. Annual sales of $100K. Handle own marketing, purchasing, and bookkeeping.
- Began operation from scratch and realized profit after first year.
- Planned office design for—and successfully completed 48-hour relocation of—computer software company, including moving mainframe and computer terminals.
- Provided consultation, design, and purchases for two 200-seat specialty restaurants, including all components of dining area, such as wall cover, flooring, seating, dinnerware, and all decorations.
- Supervised $100K home addition, including consultation on construction materials, windows, ceilings, lighting, flooring, furniture, and window-cover selections.

1995-2000

Designer, Restaurants, Etc., Cincinnati, Ohio
Served as interior designer for company specializing in cafeterias for large office buildings. Produced elevations, floor plans, and reflected ceiling plans.
- Provided consultation on materials in kitchen construction, such as walls, floors, ceilings and lighting.
- Planned and purchased all components of dining area, including wall cover, flooring, seating, tables, dinnerware, cutlery, and all decorations.
- Planned and supervised $100K food court for shopping mall.
- Designed cafeteria for Justice Center in County Court building.
- Planned and designed interior for $225K, 400-seat restaurant.

WORK EXPERIENCE

1992-1995	**Designer, Meredith Willing & Co., Cincinnati, Ohio** One of five designers with privately owned enterprise. Worked with 8 to 10 residential clients annually on a variety of projects ranging from $3-350K. Produced elevations, floor plans, and sketches for all projects. ■ Determined lighting and selected appropriate fixtures. ■ Handled color and fabric schemes and furniture selections. ■ Expanded company's client base 25%. ■ Helped plan and oversee $350K home addition, including working with the architect and contractor; planned every aspect of interiors for exercise room, children's playroom, and in-home bar.
1990-1992	**Purchasing/Contract Specialist, Thomas Interiors, Inc., Cincinnati, Ohio** Worked for design company with more than 200 commercial clients and $6M in annual sales. Handled correspondence with clients. ■ Wrote sales contracts up to $250K. ■ Developed price quotes for sales contracts and generated purchase orders for goods and services in contracts.
1988-1990	**Manufacturer's Manager, The Mart, Cincinnati, Ohio** Represented 25 manufacturers in showroom. Provided information to—and completed sales with—architects and designers. ■ Began as salesperson in retail showroom, promoted to manager after eight months. ■ Handled furniture, carpeting and flooring, fabrics, and lighting.

EDUCATION

1988	Bachelor's Degree in Fine Arts, University of Cincinnati, Ohio Major: Interior Design Minors: Ceramics, Drawing

AFFILIATIONS

1994-present	Member, American Society of Interior Designers
1999-present	Director, Greater Cincinnati Home-A-Rama Showcase

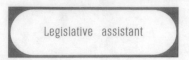
JOHN L. MARTIN

951 Ford Rd. ▶ Alexandria, VA ▶ 22392 ▶ (703) 555-2442 ▶ MartinJ@mycomp.net

SUMMARY OF QUALIFICATIONS

▶ Seven years experience in constituent relations, legislative research, and evaluation.

▶ Solid background in public event planning, scheduling, and coordination.

▶ Skilled in researching and preparing issue- and event-related briefing material.

▶ Experienced in campaign management, including successful fund-raising programs.

WORK EXPERIENCE

Legislative Assistant, U.S. Senator Steven Knight of Massachusetts, Washington, DC (2001-present)

Serve as liaison between Senator Knight and constituents on agriculturally related legislation.

▶ Manage agricultural-specific projects and draft comprehensive reviews of projects and legislation.

▶ Established "town meetings" between Senator and constituents, which provide Input and insight into current issues and concerns.

▶ Manage constituent correspondence and arrange tours of Capitol.

Advanceman, Governor William Tollifson, State of Massachusetts, Boston, MA (1999-2001)

Traveled with governor to all public events and maintained governor's schedule.

▶ Compiled information about top concerns and issues for each locale/event.

▶ Managed constituent requests and prepared follow-up correspondence.

Campaign Staff, William Tollifson for Governor, Boston (1998-1999)

▶ Chaired fund-raising committee, which increased number of donors from 2,000 to 12,000 and raised more than $2 million in campaign contributions through direct solicitation, direct mail, events, and receptions.

▶ Assisted in volunteer coordination.

Schedule Coordinator, Massachusetts Democratic State Committee, Boston (1996-1998)

Coordinated public events schedules for four state candidates and office holders.

▶ Prospected events for candidates, which increased their visibility and enhanced their public image.

▶ Organized and directed five-day, 30-city campaign bus tour.

Legislative/Administrative Intern, Massachusetts Trial Lawyers Association (MTLA), Boston (1995-1996)

▶ Maintained and updated computerized and hard-copy records of more than 500 pieces of legislation.

▶ Analyzed and evaluated more than 1,000 pages of legal decisions, statutes, and civil codes.

▶ Prepared evaluations and reports for House and Senate committees and the MTLA Board of Directors.

EDUCATION

Bachelor of Arts in Political Science, Massachusetts University, Boston (1995)

Elizabeth Moriarty

62 Eastgate Ct.
Windmere, GA 30998
(404) 555-9023
www.EJM_page.net

Summary of Skills

➤ Experienced in creating innovative programs to involve children in their local library and instill the love of books in children, teachers, and parents.
➤ Skilled in public speaking and communicating information about library programs.
➤ Thorough knowledge of children's books, reference materials, audio-visual collections, and reading/activity computer software.
➤ Adept in budget management, purchasing, and supervising volunteers.
➤ Strong computer skills.

Professional Experience

Head Librarian, Children's Department, Carnegie Public Library, Windmere, GA 2000 - present

Conduct all children's story-telling and special programs. Work with local teachers to help meet instructional needs. Visit local pre-schools, 4-H and Scout meetings, and other children's organizations to introduce programs and encourage participation. Order and maintain library collection and track computerized budget.

➤ Initiated library's bar code system for automated check-out, returns, and inventory, resulting in more accurate records, improved inventory, and faster check-out/check-in.
➤ Established Jr. Volunteer program for middle school students to reduce heavy demands on paid staff and introduce students to library operations; volunteers have enhanced operations by reshelving books in a more timely manner, assisting younger patrons with computer skills, and helping plan special children's programs.
➤ Advise student volunteers on Children's Department newsletter, which is distributed to all patrons; newsletter has improved students' computer and communications skills and won recognition from the Georgia Library Association.
➤ Plan special holiday programs to increase involvement and encourage younger patrons to visit library on regular basis.
➤ Received library board grant and established children's computer center to enhance computer skills and provide learning opportunity through educational software.

Professional Experience

Assistant Librarian, Children's Department, Carnegie Public Library, Windmere, GA
1997 - 2000
- Created children's summer reading program, which nearly doubled the number of young patrons visiting the library.
- Initiated special weekly summer programs, such as arts and crafts, puppet shows, juggling and magic exhibitions, train excursions, author visits, games, and music.
- Established weekly Wee Ones story time for 18- to 36-month-old children and Story Time for children ages 3 to 6; after one year, expanded to bi-weekly session to accommodate interested young readers.
- Initiated "Young Puppeteers" for middle-school students, which enhanced their story-telling and creative skills as they presented quarterly puppet shows for elementary-aged children.

Related Experience

Chairman, Children's & Young People's Division, Georgia Library Association
2000 - 2002
Planned annual fall conference, including researching and hiring speakers and talent, and arranging accommodations and meals. Created and distributed registration/informational brochure.
- Presented session on how to get the most out of youth volunteers without driving them away.
- Initiated "share and compare" session, where attendees exchanged handouts, brochures, and flyers to learn about other programming ideas they could use in their own libraries, resulting in more creative programming in all state public libraries.
- Secured corporate sponsor, which reduced registration fees and allowed more members to attend.

Volunteer Librarian, Burrows Elementary School, Windmere, GA
1994 - 1996
Assisted school librarian in reshelving and checking out books and helping students find materials.
- Tutored nearly 20 children in reading.
- Recommended "Book Buddies" program, which enhanced children's literacy by encouraging them to read about a variety of subjects in pairs and present brief reports to their classmates; students won awards based on the number of books read.

Education/Licensing

B.A. in Humanities, Georgia State University, Atlanta (1987)

State of Georgia Children's Specialist License (1999)

Dennis K. Ruddell • 6521 N. County Line Rd. • Gaithersburg, IL • 60221 • (708) 555-3551

Summary of Qualifications

Extensive background in rural housing and agricultural loans, appraisal and financial planning. Skilled in developing loan packages with sound financial plans, realistic cash flows, and proper security. Experienced in public administration and handling government contracts. Adept in communicating information about government programs to the public. Excellent supervisory, organizational, analytical, and computer skills.

Work Experience

Agricultural Management Specialist—County Supervisor, United States Department of Agriculture—Farmers Home Administration
Gaithersburg, IL (1999 - present)
Wawaset, IL (1997 - 1999)

- Approve loans up to $360,000.
- Properly manage, service, and maintain loan portfolio of approximately $32 million, representing 90 farm and 410 housing borrowers.
- Work with delinquent and insolvent borrowers to defer, reschedule, re-amortize, consolidate, write down, or liquidate loans.
- Cooperate with other lending institutions on subordinations, releases, and FmHA guaranteed loans.
- Manage acquired property involving maintenance, repair, lease, and sale, usually through government contracts.
- Manage office and seven-person staff covering six central Illinois counties.
- Initiated and received department/government approval to upgrade computer system and software, resulting in easier information retrieval and analysis and more informative financial report generation.

Agricultural Assistant to the County Supervisor, United States Department of Agriculture Farmers Home Administration, Mulberry, IL
(1995 - 1997)

- Recommended for approval and serviced rural housing and agricultural loans.
- Appraised real and chattel security property.
- Implemented new government program for borrowers involved in bankruptcy proceedings, resulting in faster closings, less paper work, and less government contract work.
- Initiated quarterly meetings with local farmers and agribusiness representatives to explain changes in state and federal laws and regulations, enhancing customer service and enabling farm owners/operators to establish successful businesses.

Assistant Farm Manager and Rural Appraiser, Taylor Land Services, Springfield, Illinois
(1993 - 1995)

- Assisted in farm management.
- Handled preliminary preparation of rural real estate appraisals.
- Assisted in accounting, payables, receivables, bookkeeping, payroll, and preparation of technical documents and reports.
- Recommended updated accounting system, which provided a more customer-oriented financial analysis, enhancing customer service.

Work Experience

Student Staff Assistant, University of Illinois, Vocational Agriculture Services, Urbana, Illinois
(1990 - 1993)
- Assisted in billing and record-keeping.
- Developed microcomputer programs for accounting and office purposes, resulting in more accurate bookkeeping and improved analysis.
- Worked in all areas of agriculture through sales and production of agricultural education materials.

Integrated Pest Management Scout, Warren County Cooperative Extension, Westfield, Ohio
(Summer 1993)
- Solely responsible for scouting 35 farms in central Ohio.
- Checked corn, soybean, and alfalfa fields for insect, weed, and disease damage, and completed soil and tissue sampling and testing.
- Reported findings to farmers and Extension Service.

Education

Bachelor of Science Degree in Agricultural Economics (1993)
University of Illinois, College of Agriculture, Urbana

Honors

- FmHA County Office of the Year (1999)
- FmHA Certificate of Outstanding Accomplishment (1998)
- FmHA Certificate of Merit (1997)
- Administrative Point of Light for Community Service with Farm Safety for Just Kids Program (1998)

Volunteer Activities

Organizing Director, Green County Farm Safety for Just Kids Day Camp
(1999 - present)
- Established farm safety program for children, including presentations from local law enforcement and emergency medical services, farm owners/operators, and agricultural chemical representatives.
- Handle all public relations and coordinate up to 25 volunteers.
- Secure sponsorships so program can be offered free-of-charge to participants.

Other Affiliations

President, Optimist Club of Gaithersburg (2001 - present)
Treasurer, Green County Young Farmers (2000 - present)

Greg Timmons

901 East South Street
Bloomfield, MI 48550
(517) 555-6676

Summary of Skills

Generator repair and maintenance
Electric pallet jack repair
Freezer maintenance
Rapidstand conveyer repair and maintenance
Ammonia systems experience
Heavy equipment repair and maintenance
Basic residential and commercial construction knowledge
Supervisory experience
Electric drill

Can also operate:
Loboy
Forklift
Backhoe
Bulldozer
Circular saw
Electric staple gun

Employment Record

Mitchell's Grocery, Downtown Warehouse, Bloomfield, MI (1996-present)
- Supervise all phases of building maintenance, oversee staff of three.
- Recommended new preventive maintenance procedure, which reduced machinery downtime and nearly eliminated hourly overtime wages.

Smith and Bright Contractors, Ann Arbor, MI (1990-1996)
- Managed 25 pieces of equipment and crew of 12.
- Worked on residential and commercial projects.
- Initiated crew rotation schedule, which increased on-time project completion without increasing wage expenses.

Lawrence and Sons Builders, Washington, MI (1985-1990)
- Provided general labor for residential construction.
- Researched and recommended new roofing product, which provided the high-quality results the builder required at a savings of 20% over the product the builder had used.

Education

Graduate, Truman High School, Applegate, MI (1983)

Military Service

U.S. Army (1983 - 1985)
- Served on construction crew for civil engineering unit.

TIMOTHY L. HINSHAW
111 Wilshire Dr.
Memphis, TN 38127
(901) 555-0990   TLHins@mailbox.net   Cell: (901) 555-2044

SKILLS SUMMARY   Excellent technical experience with strong background in mechanical engineering applications. Experienced in new facility set-up and management. Proven track record of exceeding all production, quality and cost goals. Trained and experienced in current quality engineering methods.

CAREER HISTORY

Manufacturing Manager, Hopewell Enterprises, Memphis, TN   2000 - present
Start up and manage manufacturing and assembly facility for entrepreneurial company. Supervise production, engineering, human resources and maintenance. Design and implement optimum manufacturing processes for new products. Understand and comply with UL, FDA, and NSF regulations.

- Designed, organized, and set up new manufacturing facility below budget and ahead of schedule.
- Exceed all production, quality, and cost goals in a fast-paced entrepreneurial environment.
- Serve as technical expert on all critical operations, which has resulted in improved production, assembly, and quality processes.

Process Engineer, Worldwide Coatings, Knoxville, TN   1997 - 2000
Provided leadership and engineering solutions to technically complex problems and barriers. Designed and built new coating cells using the latest technology.

- Took charge of $500 million capital investment project to design/install three manufacturing cells in new plant.
- Recognized for developing new business growth.

Assistant Engineer, Worldwide Coatings, Knoxville, TN   1996 - 1997
Assisted in managing production, scheduling, and training. Promoted in one year for rapidly handling assigned duties and aggressively seeking more responsibility.

- Developed and supervised processes for new product, which helped exceed projected production goals.

EDUCATION   B.S., Mechanical Engineering, with honors, University of Tennessee, Memphis (1996)

Claire E. Hudson
24 Stoneycreek Drive ✦ Columbus, IL ✦ 61002 ✦ (815) 555-2934 ✦ Claireehu@alo.com

Skills Profile   Professional with eight years experience in the healthcare industry, including marketing, project management, needs assessment, and education. Experienced in developing programs and budgets, coordinating and training volunteers,
and securing grants. Skilled in media and public relations, including creating brochures and writing press releases. Proficient in computer graphics software.

Work Experience

2000 - present   **Marketing Director, Center for Hand and Foot Surgery, Peoria, IL**
Developed and maintain referral base of physicians and other healthcare providers. Develop annual work plan and budget for marketing areas. Orient new staff on office procedures and computerized scheduling system.
- ✦ Coordinate and negotiate contracts with managed care networks, resulting in an increased network of care givers who must meet specific professional standards.
- ✦ Developed tools for patient satisfaction and outcomes measurement, which has led to three new successful programs to address patient needs.
- ✦ Serve as primary contact for all media-related and public-awareness projects.
- ✦ Coordinate support groups and professional education seminars.
- ✦ Produce flyers and brochures to inform patients and the public about the center's services, and educate the public about qualified healthcare.

1997 - 2000   **Vice President, Programs and Services, Multiple Sclerosis Foundation, Illinois Chapter, Peoria, IL**
Developed annual objectives and budget for program-related areas. Hired and supervised program assistant. Served as primary contact for all media-related projects and press conferences.
- ✦ Designed new volunteer recruitment program, which increased the number of volunteers statewide by 40%.
- ✦ Trained more than 200 volunteer instructors annually for MS programs.
- ✦ Wrote and edited monthly press releases and quarterly newsletters.
- ✦ Secured financial underwriting for projects, including annual telethon, which helped finance state education programs, free clinics, and special events.

1994 - 1997   **Health Education Consultant, Crawford County Health Department, Westin, IL**
- ✦ Secured grants for and coordinated community health needs assessment, which identified three major areas of concern.
- ✦ Designed programs to address assessment needs and organized appropriate health education programs and volunteers throughout the county.
- ✦ Conducted follow-up assessment, which found nearly 75% improvement in two of the identified areas and 55% improvement in the third.

Education   B.A. in Pubic Health, University of Illinois, Urbana/Champaign (1994)

YEE SU WONG

5216 Stone Ridge Rd.
Princeton, NJ 08544
609·555·3111
609·555·4763 (Cell Phone)
YeesuWong@mailbox.net

SKILLS SUMMARY   Nearly 15 years marketing experience with insurance and benefits. Skilled in creating innovative programs for corporate markets. Adept in developing products and programs across corporate lines. Solid background in developing products for benefits programs.

CAREER HISTORY

Vice President—Marketing, Hunter & Associates, Inc., Princeton, NJ   **2000-present**

Senior marketing officer for general insurance underwriter. Handle marketing and sales of all product lines, including stop loss health re-insurance, group life, flexible benefits, and ancillary products. Manage all personnel and functions for six field offices.

- Managed premium growth to an annual rate of $64 million.
- Established new distribution system to increase flexible benefits software and administration sales, while realizing revenue from related individual product sales.

Manager—Corporate Sales, National Life Insurance Company, New York, NY   **1996-2000**

Managed sales in large corporation market, primarily through brokerage sources, by taking advantage of emerging market opportunities.

- Created innovative programs for corporate markets, such as integrating group and individual products, which helped expand client base.
- Expanded number of brokerage outlets and increased production from current brokers through relationship marketing, seminars, and advertising.

Manager—Marketing, National Life Insurance Company, New York, NY   **1994-1996**
Managed all marketing functions for 70 agencies and 1,500 agents, including advanced sales, training, payroll deduction plans, product promotion, and incentives. Managed staff of 25 and $6 million budget.

- ▶ Designed and introduced new policy, which realized $15 million premium in its first two years.
- ▶ Introduced and edited agency newsletter, which provided sales/marketing information, helped close communication gap between home and field offices, and provided consistency in information.

Manager—Marketing Operations, Pennsylvania Life, Philadelphia, PA   **1990-1994**
Managed all sales-support areas, including advanced sales, management recruiting, training, and conventions, for independent brokerage. Supervised staff of 15 and $1.5 million budget.

- ▶ Designed and launched six major new products in three years, generating 1993 premium revenue of more than $50 million.

Supervisor—Product Sales, Pennsylvania Life, Philadelphia, PA   **1989-1990**
Supervised advanced sales, product promotion, and incentive program. Worked with 800 field agents. Handled all communication with field staff. Supervised office staff of three.

- ▶ Established incentive program for two new products, which generated premium revenue of more than $5 million.
- ▶ Initiated new marketing team, which designed short- and long-term goals for all life products.

EDUCATION   B.S., Business Administration,
                       University of Kentucky, Louisville, *with honors* (1989)

MEMBERSHIPS   Association for Advanced Life Underwriting (AALU)
                       National Association of Life Underwriters (NALU)

JEANETTE D. McCANN, PH.D.

33 Westview Dr.
Wilmington, DE 19899
DrJeanette@quick.net

(302) 555-3994

Cell: (302) 555-7217

PROFILE

Skilled technical manager with doctorate in materials and more than six years of project management experience. Excellent background in planning and directing technical efforts, in manufacturing process development, and in product improvement programs. Strong analytical and investigative skills.

PROFESSIONAL EXPERIENCE

1996 - present

Willow Technical Systems, Wilmington, DE
Senior Materials Engineer
Direct all technical activity on internally funded multi-year product development/process optimization programs. Forecast, budget, and schedule program milestones for all programs. Manage annual program budget of more than $800,000. Supervise nine engineers.

➤ Serve as in-house focal point for materials and processing issues and establish procedures that enhance production coordination and increase productivity.

➤ Serve as project engineer for customer and government-funded materials/process development programs and coordinate engineering functions to successfully meet customer schedule and budget requirements.

➤ Established coordination components for company-wide functions, which help move projects toward defined goals and enhance ability to meet customer needs, budgets and schedules.

➤ Revised application of high-strength steels, advanced aluminum alloys, metal and polymer composites, and ceramics in aerospace products, resulting in improved product performance and increased sales.

➤ Developed process that concentrated on casting methods, thermal and mechanical treatments, powder metallurgy, joining methods, and machining and grinding, which provided the opportunity to develop new products and markets.

➤ Directed high-performance material assessment, including material characterization for design, damage tolerance, and fracture mechanics, which improved manufacturing process and product development.

PROFESSIONAL EXPERIENCE

1993 - 1996   **Mayfair Incorporated, Wilmington, DE**
Research Engineer
Managed projects for several externally sponsored and company-funded manufacturing development programs. Presented program highlights at executive conferences and trade shows.

- ➤ Emphasized the material's influence on optimal processing methods, resulting in improved manufacturing processes and products.
- ➤ Handled the entire spectrum of the traditional material removal processes, nonconventional techniques, tool design, process design, and expert systems.
- ➤ Revised research process to better coordinate with product marketing, resulting in more successful marketing programs and increased sales.

EDUCATION

Doctorate of Materials Science and Engineering,
University of Delaware (1994)
Dissertation topic: Alloy modifications to Deotel 61 to reduce additions of strategic elements while retaining the original material properties.

Master of Science, University of Delaware (1992)
Thesis topic: Optimizing the structure and properties of advanced cast irons to improve thermal fatigue resistance.

Bachelor of Science, University of Delaware (1990)

PUBLICATIONS

Doctoral Dissertation
McCann, *Metallurgy and Properties Research*, Pressman Publishers, 1997

Master's Thesis
McCann, *National Foundryman's Journal*, Wolcott & Associates, 1993

Invited Papers/Presentations
"Cutting Tool Geometry Effects on the Machining of Aerospace
    Materials," 1997 International Machine Tool Show, Chicago, IL
"Composite Materials in Torpedo Propulsion Systems,"
    2002 American Defense Preparedness Association, Bern, CA

Medical transcriptionist

Michael Nasser • 323 Oak Drive • Edenberg, IL • 60016 • (708) 555-3554

Summary of Qualifications

Thorough knowledge of medical terminology, with good understanding of surgical and laboratory procedures. Efficient with WordPerfect and medical transcription software on IBM or compatible system. Ability to type 85 words per minute with high degree of accuracy. Possess necessary equipment and reference materials to work from home. Experienced in medical office management.

Work Experience

Medical Transcriptionist, Columbus General Hospital, Columbus, IL
2001 - present
- Transcribe for coronary, neurology, orthopedic, psychiatric, and internal medicine physicians in 100-plus physician hospital.
- Evaluated and recommended hiring three part-time transcriptionists to work from their homes instead of hiring two full-time transcriptionists, saving $22,000 annually in wages and benefits.

Office Manager, Hand Surgery Institute, Columbus, IL
1999 - 2001
- Handled payroll, bookkeeping, and office scheduling for two surgeons.
- Supervised clinic's insurance clerk, front desk receptionist, and part-time transcriptionist.
- Established patient payment plan program, which decreased late payments and uncollectibles by 75%.

Transcriptionist/Coder, Chemical Dependency Center, Crawfordsville, IL
1997 - 1999
- Transcribed medical information for more than 100 patients.
- Assigned international medical procedure codes to patient records for insurance purposes.

Records Clerk, Crawfordsville Medical Clinic, Crawfordsville, IL
1996 - 1997
- Handled documentation, storage, and retrieval of medical information for four physicians.
- Assisted with front office/reception duties.
- Evaluated and recommended computerized record keeping, supervised all data entry, and generated reports for planning and budgeting.

Education

Lincoln Tech Vocational Institute, Peoria, IL (1995 - 1996)
- Medical transcription
- Medical coding
- Medical terminology

Memberships

National Health Professions Association

THERESA A. LUTZ
51 N. Black Hill Dr.
Rapid City, SD 57709
605·555·9883; 605·555·1020 (Cell Phone)

PROFILE

▸ Nearly 10 years of experience in developing community resources, recruiting professional and volunteer personnel, and operating efficiently and effectively within budget constraints.
▸ Solid background in securing grants from proposal stage through reporting on compliance and financial issues.
▸ Effective public relations skills, including delivering formal presentations, written communications, and planning and conducting fund-raising campaigns.

WORK EXPERIENCE

Executive Director, Sioux County Senior Services, Inc., Black Hills, S.Dak. (1995-present)

Supervise organization's service program and daily operations. Work closely with board of directors and carry out policies and programs. Supervise five full-time and 10 part-time employees. Develop programs, solicit funds, recruit board members, and train staff members. Oversee two annual fund-raising events.

▸ Formed not-for-profit entity in 1995 to coordinate needed senior services.
▸ Built organization into valuable service provider with more than 275 volunteers who offer up to 20 services (such as homemaking, home healthcare, and tax and insurance assistance) to more than 2,500 seniors in the community.
▸ Prepare federal, state, and private grant proposals with high record of acceptance.
▸ Plan and administer $325,000 annual budget.
▸ Established respite care program, which provides relief to family members caring for homebound seniors through qualified volunteers.

Volunteer Coordinator, Arrow County Senior Services, Elgin, Wyo. (1993-1995)

Worked with and scheduled up to 150 volunteers annually to provide variety of services to county's senior citizens. Edited "50 plus" section in local newspaper.

▸ Secured donated vehicles and scheduled volunteer drivers to establish transportation service.
▸ Implemented hearing and health screenings for seniors at local fairs and festivals.
▸ Implemented organization's first Christmas tree fund raiser, which realized nearly $2,000 in profit annually.
▸ Increased number of volunteers 75% during tenure.
▸ Established referral system for seniors in need of counseling, tax assistance, insurance assistance, and more.

WORK EXPERIENCE

Second Grade Teacher, Elgin Public Schools, Elgin, Wyo. (1991-1995)

Provided appropriate curriculum, guidance and hands-on experiences for 22 children. Provided regular feedback to parents on children's progress. Coordinated and scheduled all field trips for four 2nd- and 3rd-grade classes.

▸ Worked with administration to establish new guidelines for textbook selection, which improved quality of materials in elementary education classrooms.

▸ Created volunteer pool to assist with math and reading tutoring during classroom hours, which provided additional assistance to students and increased parental involvement.

▸ Researched adding computers to elementary education classrooms and helped plan September 1995 implementation.

EDUCATION/CERTIFICATION

B.S. in Elementary Education, Wyoming University, Cheyenne (1991)

Counseling Courses, South Dakota University, Rapid City (1997-1999)

Certified Home Economist in Human Services (1996)

ACTIVITIES

President, Zonta International Businesswomen's Association, Rapid City

Volunteer, Rapid City Children's Choir

Nurse

Rhonda Spencer

16354 Dover Lane
Mountain Springs, CO 80445

(303) 555-9009
RhondaS@mail.net

Summary of Qualifications

Award-winning registered nurse with strong background in supervision and all areas of patient care. Ten years of experience in CCU, ICU, medical and surgical progressive, general medical-surgical, orthopedics, home care, and more. Also experienced in developing and implementing a variety of hospital patient care and employee training programs.

Work Experience

RN Case Manager, Home Health Services of General Hospital, Denver, CO   **2000-present**
- Manage total care needs for up to 30 patients (per week) in their homes.
- Supervise six Home Health Aides (HHAs).
- Plan and direct necessary additional training for aides, including annual CPR certification.
- Created brochure explaining hospital's home care program and how it benefits patients and their families, increasing number of clients by 35%.
- Developed and implemented hospital-based HHA training program to address demand for home aides, resulting in increased staff and increased opportunities to meet community needs.

Housewide Float RN, General Hospital, Denver, CO   **1998-2000**
- Quality care-giver in CCU, ICU, medical progressive, surgical progressive, general medical-surgical, orthopedics, post-partum, med-psych, and newborn nursery.
- Revamped hospital's "New Mom/New Baby" patient information program and developed take-home package, which provided essential information and educational materials for new mothers on 24-hour stay.

General Post-Surgical RN, General Hospital, Denver, CO   **1996-1998**
- Cared for post-op patients, including EKG tracings, aerosol treatments and chest percussion, phlebotomy and lab test preparation, quality review and insurance recertification.

GYN/Oncology RN, Cooper Memorial Hospital, Colorado Springs, CO   **1995-1996**
- Cared for routine GYN post-surgery patients and GYN oncology patients.
- Administered chemotherapy and cared for routine post-partum and C-section patients.
- Developed hospital's "Family Care" support group program to address needs of family members of oncology patients, resulting in greater understanding of—and better ability to cope with—a terminally ill family member.

Work Experience

CCU RN, Cooper Memorial Hospital, Colorado Springs, CO   **1994-1996**
> ➤ Handled basic and advanced EKG interpretation, care of pre- and post-catheterization patients, care of pre- and post-PTCA patients, intraortic balloon pump (IABP) monitoring, cardiac output monitoring, Swan Ganz catheter and arterial line care and monitoring, and pre- and post-coronary artery bypass graft (CABG) patients.

Emergency Department RN, Cooper Memorial Hospital, Colorado Springs, CO   **1993-1994**
> ➤ Helped develop program to familiarize probationary (still in training) firefighters and EMTs with emergency room procedures, resulting in better informed EMS staffs and enhancing emergency room operations.

CCU RN, Cooper Memorial Hospital, Colorado Springs, CO   **1992-1993**
> ➤ Served on committee that assessed patient visitation hours and wrote committee report to department head, which led to changes to better meet patient and family needs.

Student Nurse Extern, Colorado University Medical Center, Freemont, CO   **1991-1992**
> ➤ Cared for patients in all areas of the hospital.
> ➤ Delivered thank-you speech on behalf of all student nurses at annual hospital staff banquet.

Education/Certification

ANA Med-Surg Nursing Certificate (1996)
B.S. in Nursing, Colorado University, Freemont (1993)
SON Diploma, Colorado University Medical Center, Freemont (1989-1992)
General Studies, Mountain State University, Mountain Springs, CO (1988-1989)

Professional Organizations/ Awards

2002   Secretary, Colorado Alliance for Home Health Care
2001   Outstanding RN Case Manager Award, General Hospital, Denver, CO
2000   Partner of the Year in Quality Care Award, General Hospital, Denver, CO

SUSAN FORD

1556 River Road ✦ Talleyville, KS ✦ 66014 ✦ (913) 555-0332 ✦ Sueford@access.net

SKILLS PROFILE

- ✦ Six years of office supervisory experience.
- ✦ Skilled in developing successful office procedures.
- ✦ Experienced in establishing collection plans and monitoring collection activity.
- ✦ Accustomed to working in a fast-paced environment and successfully handling several responsibilities simultaneously.

EMPLOYMENT HISTORY

Office Supervisor, William G. Morse, MD, Talleyville, KS (1999-present)
- ✦ Manage operation and maintenance of office equipment, maintain appropriate quantities of business supplies, and maintain cost records and supply sources for all business supplies.
- ✦ Established office payment plan program; arrange payment plans with patients; monitor those accounts to ensure compliance; prepare monthly report detailing collection activity; uncollected payments have fallen by 25%.
- ✦ Perform administrative tasks such as distributing the mail, scheduling meetings, and typing letters and documents.
- ✦ Created and continue to update written job descriptions for office personnel.
- ✦ Developed manual for all business office procedures, resulting in standardized operations.
- ✦ Schedule daily appointments, handle phone communication, greet patients, collect payments, and post accurate record of office charges and receipts into computer.

Office Manager, Kevin D. McPherson, DDS, Knots, KS (1997-1999)
- ✦ Performed business office duties, including payroll, accounts payable and accounts receivable, and balanced all accounts monthly.
- ✦ Filed insurance claims and handled carrier requests.
- ✦ Represented doctor's office in small claims court when filing against nonpaying clients.
- ✦ Developed and maintained patient confirmation and no-show policies, which decreased no-shows by 50%.

Receptionist, Kevin D. McPherson, DDS, Knots, KS (1996-1997)
- ✦ Scheduled daily appointments and handled phone communication.
- ✦ Retrieved and filed charts for each day's patients; prepared new patient charts.
- ✦ Collected and posted payments.

Sales Clerk, Cramer Furniture, Talleyville, KS (1995-1996)
- ✦ Handled floor sales in lamps and dining room furniture.
- ✦ Assisted with credit reporting, collections, bookkeeping, and installment contracts.
- ✦ Helped develop special sales and promotion plans, which led to 20% sales increase.

EDUCATION

Kansas Technical/Vocational College, Kansas City (1995-1997)
    Related courses: accounting, computer operations, business communications
Warren County High School, Crown Point, KS (Graduated 1995)

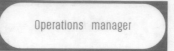

Cynthia J. Snyder

215 Kelley Rd. • Honolulu, HI • 96845 • (808) 555-9804 • CJS_OT@mailuser.net

Summary of Qualifications

Engineer and manager with seven years production and operations experience. Skilled in team building and in implementing employee involvement and quality-control programs to increase morale and performance. Proven track record of exceeding production, quality, safety, and financial goals.

Professional Experience

Operations Manager, TileTex, Inc., Honolulu, HI
(2000-present)
Manage and control manufacturing facility. Handle processes, procedures, human resources, and financial performance. Work with limited administrative support, which requires ability to "wear all hats." Serve as liaison with headquarters's corporate staff and sales team in Chicago.

- Recommended use for manufacturing by-product that has generated nearly $2 million annually in sales.
- Established fully computerized operations with Chicago office, saving $20,000 annually in telephone and facsimile expenses.
- Initiated one-on-one review process with top customers to ensure customer satisfaction and meet or exceed quality standards; have retained 100% of the customers.

Production Supervisor, Suprex Industries, Honolulu, HI
(1995-2000)
Supervised production, scheduling, and training activities and assisted production manager in cooperation/support of joint venture customers. Provided technical leadership.

- Initiated use of Total Quality Control and Employee Involvement programs to achieve highest output in 12 years (65% increase over previous year).
- Managed start up of new facility, implemented team concept, and achieved performance standards that exceeded first-year goal by 20%.
- Commended by division president for creating/leading teams, supervising successful new plant start up, and exceeding production, quality, and safety standards.

Education

Bachelor of Science in Mechanical Engineering, *Magna Cum Laude,*
Case Western Reserve University, Cleveland, OH (1995)

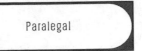

Paralegal

SANDRA CHEN LU

95 W. Kimmel St.
Glenview, CA 92332

(619) 555-2440 (home)
(619) 555-2009 (work)

SUMMARY OF SKILLS

- Extensive legal experience in product liability, medical malpractice, contracts, real estate, and personal injury litigation.
- Trained and experienced in photography and in investigation and interviewing techniques.
- Capable of working quickly and accurately under pressure to successfully meet short deadlines.
- Able to analyze complex and detailed material and solve problems.
- Effective oral and written communication skills.
- Strong computer skills, including detailed knowledge of WordPerfect and PageMaker.

EDUCATION/CERTIFICATION

1997	NALA Certified Legal Assistant
1997	Certificate, California State University Paralegal Program
1998	Certificate, Litigation and Trial Practice, The Paralegal Institute
1999	Courses in Private Investigating and Photography, California State University Continuing Education Program
2000	Courses is Computer Software and Real Estate, Valley Vocational College, Springfield, CA

PROFESSIONAL EXPERIENCE

1997-present **Litigation Paralegal, Warren, Pauley & Underhill, Glenview, CA**
- Interview clients, witnesses, and experts to gather information for trial.
- Prepare legal documents and settlement brochures.
- Gather and interpret medical records and reports and provide written evaluation for attorneys.
- Attend trials with litigation attorneys to provide information and assistance.
- Research issues and cases and report findings to attorneys.
- Investigated and discovered vital information for five $8M-$30M medical malpractice cases, two of which were well-publicized litigations; firm won all five cases.
- Interviewed experts, reviewed documentation and completed legal research for three $15M- $50M product class action cases; firm won all three cases.

PROFESSIONAL AFFILIATIONS

2000-present Secretary, Treasurer, California Paralegal Association, Inc.
1998-present President, Treasurer, Glen County Legal Personnel
2002-present San Diego Bar Association

AMANDA WOODFIELD

19 E. Lansing Dr.
Tidewater, VA 23033
(804) 555-2993
Fax: (804) 555-2994
AWoodfield@hayoo.com

SKILLS SUMMARY

Pharmacist with more than 10 years of experience, including extensive background in administering government programs. Skilled in developing record-keeping and patient profile systems and creating in-service training programs. Experienced in preparing budgets and monthly department reports. Experienced in serving as consultant to various medical staffs on medication interactions, adverse effects, and appropriate dosages.

EMPLOYMENT

Pharmacist, Rehabilitation Center, Virginia Bureau of Worker's Compensation, Tidewater, VA (2000-present)

Accurately order and distribute medications to clients and provide client counseling in accordance with VBRA 40. Develop and implement wean schedules for clients, helping them to reduce and eventually eliminate medication use. Prepare and conduct in-service training for staff. Prepare fiscal year budget and monthly reports.

- ➤ Developed record-keeping system for pharmacy, including new forms for tracking medication received, distributed, and returned, resulting in more accurate records and improved inventory control.
- ➤ Created new patient profile system for pharmacy, which allowed for review of accurate, up-to-date patient profiles to determine medication interactions, adverse effects, and appropriate dosages.
- ➤ Established physician signature card process, reducing physician approval delays by 35%.
- ➤ Created protocol for contingency cabinet, which established detailed operating procedures and eliminated unwarranted use.

**Pharmacist, Support Services, Virginia Department of Mental Health, Tidewater, VA
(1996-2000)**

Accurately dispensed psychotropic medication to outpatient mental health agencies throughout Virginia in a timely manner. Reviewed patient profiles for medication interactions, adverse effects, and appropriate dosages using both manual and computerized processing system.

➤ Supervised final phase of data entry from manual to computerized system, resulting in increased productivity, improved record keeping, and enhanced inventory summaries.

➤ Initiated and conducted training sessions covering changes in state and federal pharmacy laws and newly marketed medications, ensuring compliance and resulting in a well-informed staff.

➤ Maintained well-controlled inventory, including legally handling and storing controlled substances.

**Staff Pharmacist, Nursing Center Services, Virginia Department of Mental Health, Tidewater, VA
(1993-1996)**

Accepted and transcribed physician medication orders submitted by telephone from nursing home nursing staff. Checked and accurately dispensed, in a timely fashion, medication filled by pharmacy technicians.

➤ Checked unit dose medication packages for correct medication and legal labeling.

➤ Checked narcotic unit dose packages for legal labeling and storage according to Virginia state law.

➤ Created information packet concerning medication dosages, adverse effects, and interactions to help answer questions from nursing home staff, resulting in a well-informed staff and increased productivity for pharmacy.

**Staff Pharmacist, Green County Memorial Hospital, Greenville, VA
(1991-1993)**

Accurately dispensed unit dose medication according to physician orders. Maintained patient profiles with emphasis on drug interactions and dosages.

➤ Answered questions from medical staff concerning drug dosages, interactions, and adverse effects.

➤ Implemented new unit dose medication system for hospital, resulting in increased productivity and more timely delivery of medications.

EDUCATION

Bachelor of Science, Pharmacy (1991)
Virginia State University, Columbus

MIGUEL A. MARTINEZ
3330 Alden Way
Dallas, Texas 75255
MAMartinez@mymail.net

(214) 555-2002

Fax: (214) 555-9907

SKILLS PROFILE

▸ Manager with strong background in production control, machining center operations, and tooling activities.

▸ Experienced in supervising manufacturing processes, from raw material to finished product.

▸ Skilled in using a variety of precision measuring instruments and in inspection procedures.

▸ Able to effectively communicate with individuals at all levels of an organization.

EXPERIENCE
1994-present

Watkins, Inc., Dallas, Texas
Production Control Manager (2000-present)
Supervise planning, scheduling, production and shipment of products. Arrange work schedules to meet quantity and scheduling demands. Supervise more than 40 employees.

▸ Raised gross production levels 47% after 18 months, while significantly reducing man hours, errors, and waste.

▸ Respond to daily changes in customer scheduling requirements, while maintaining 0 quality defects.

▸ Recommended and implemented new production training program, which reduced training time and improved employee performance.

Production Control Supervisor (1998-2000)
Assisted manager with all control phases of production process, including supervising all inspections. Worked directly with customers to determine and meet production schedules. Supervised 10 employees.

▸ Recommended new scheduling process, which helped company raise production levels 24%.

▸ Supervised installation and start-up of new plant equipment, ensuring a smooth transition and capability to meet scheduling demands.

CNC Machining Center Set-up Operator (1994-1998)
Wrote machine programs, set up and operated LeBlond-Makino and Kitamura Mycenter machining centers.

▸ Determined points of intersection and all necessary data to manufacture quality productions to tolerances as close as ±0005.

▸ Earned Employee of the Year Award for suggestion that reorganized center would enhance workflow and increase production.

EXPERIENCE (Cont.)

1990-1994	**Texas Locks, Dallas, Texas** **Tooling Coordinator** Coordinated all tooling activities and provided support to production line. Supervised two employees.

    ▶ Redesigned tool crib, which improved workflow through better organized workstations.
    ▶ Established bin balance system.

1989-1990   **Precision Products, Dallas, Texas**
     Set-Up Operator
     Worked with multi-spindle, automatic screw machines.

    ▶ Coordinated service and warranty work with equipment companies.
    ▶ Designed new maintenance program, which reduced down-time 33% and enhanced ability to meet customer schedules.

1987-1989   **Spitz & Co., Dallas, Texas**
     Service Representative
     Installed new Mackey Automatic Multiple Spindle Screw Machines and performed on-site warranty and service at 25 Southwest plants.

    ▶ Earned company's Outstanding Customer Service Award for 1988.

EDUCATION   Riviera Community College, Riviera, Texas (1997-2000)

    ▶ 12 credit hours in management

Woodland Vocational College, Woodland, Texas (1990-1993)

    ▶ Nine credit hours in computer science
    ▶ Six credit hours in computer programming
    ▶ Six credit hours in trigonometry and pre-calculus

ACTIVITIES   Eagle Scout Leader, Troup #51, Dallas, Texas

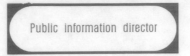

DOUGLAS R. HAUSMAN
77 E. Waverly
Durham, NC 27589
919·555·4598; (Cell Phone) 919·555·1044

SKILLS SUMMARY

Skilled communicator and manager with more than 10 years experience with state departments and agencies. Solid background in developing educational and informational programs. Adept at working with civic organizations, public officials, and citizens in addressing complaints and requests for information.

PROFESSIONAL EXPERIENCE

1998-present

Director, Public Information Office
North Carolina State Health and Environment Department
Raleigh, N.C.

Direct all public information and public affairs activities of largest department in state. Manage community and media relations, publications, and internal relations. Supervise staff of 15, including information specialists, graphic artists, and clerical support.

▷ Increased placement of news and feature articles in newspapers, magazines, and with radio and television stations by 34% in two years.

▷ Produce monthly newsletters, weekly fact sheets, brochures, public service announcements, videotape programs, displays and radio actualities, which report consistent, up-to-date information on department activities and findings.

▷ Recommended, developed, and host talk show on local radio station, which enhances department's image and increases public awareness and feedback on critical issues.

▷ Designed program that pairs civic leaders with department officials, resulting in improved communication and understanding.

1996-1998

Information Specialist, Public Affairs Office
North Carolina State Highway Department, Durham, N.C.

Wrote and edited all news releases, public service announcements, and biweekly newsletter. Wrote and produced radio actualities, public service announcements, and video programs.

▷ Initiated educational program, which emphasized department's high success rate in completing projects on schedule and within budget.

▷ Worked with state fire and law enforcement agencies to establish Emergency Communication Plan for hazardous material spills.

PROFESSIONAL EXPERIENCE

1993-1996   **Public Information Officer and Citizen Assistance Section Manager**
Virginia Environmental Protection Agency
Richmond, Va.

Managed section that responds to complaints or requests for information from citizens and public officials. Maintained close relations with state and local civic organizations and special interest groups. Wrote news and feature articles.
- Initiated and conducted community educational programs, which provided information about agency activities and how they affect the public.
- Established and maintained large research library, which provided necessary materials for public use.
- Placed more than 250 articles statewide annually, increasing coverage 45%.
- Established new tracking and follow-up system for complaints and requests for information, which led to development of two new programs to address findings and meet citizens' needs.

1990-1993   **City Editor, Managing Editor**
Millville *News Journal*
Millville, Va.

Wrote news and feature stories, primarily on city government and politics. Promoted to managing editor March 1992. Assisted in directing paper's editorial policy and supervised work of other section editors.
- Earned five Virginia State Newspaper Association Awards, including special recognition for coverage of highly contested local political race, which centered on business and environmental issues.
- Initiated and wrote column highlighting current health-related and environmental issues, which helped educate the public and increase awareness.

EDUCATION   Duke University, Raleigh/Durham, N.C. (1997-1999)
- 12 graduate credit hours in organizational behavior

University of Virginia at Richmond (1990)
- Bachelor of Arts in Political Science/Journalism

ACTIVITIES   Director, Raleigh Metropolitan Park System Board

SUSANA T. RAMIREZ

50 El Paso Drive
Dallas, TX 75202
(214) 555-3029

ST_Ramirez@powermail.com
Fax: (214) 555-2987
Work: (214) 555-7076

SKILLS SUMMARY Award-winning media relations expert with nearly 10 years of experience in virtually every aspect of public relations, including external media, customer newsletters, customer bill inserts, sponsorships, special events/ promotions, and contributions. Ability to manage a variety of media projects in creative ways. Excellent organizational, written, and communication skills. Capable of successfully managing several projects simultaneously and meeting all deadlines.

EDUCATION Master of Arts Degree in Public Relations *with honors,*
University of Texas (2000)
Bachelor of Arts Degree *with honors,* Arizona State University (1994)

EXPERIENCE

Public Relations Manager and Spokesperson, TelTech Communications, Dallas, TX   1998-present
Develop, recommend, and manage communications strategies for informing the public of regional telecommunications company's many activities throughout the state. Promote company products, service, sponsorships, and contributions. Serve as company spokesperson.

- Edit residential customer newsletter and schedule printing to meet billing cycles.
- Generated more than $50,000 worth of media coverage statewide concerning Teltech's Texan Academic Super Bowl, with more than 150 articles in newspapers throughout the state.
- Initiated TelTech's sponsorship of Yuletide Celebration, a holiday presentation by the Dallas Symphony Orchestra; sponsorship has allowed symphony to bring in special guest artists and has enhanced company's image in the art and general communities.
- Developed and implemented hometown feature program where feature articles about employees in internal company publications are placed in hometown newspapers, increasing media coverage and enhancing public image.
- Wrote and placed five articles about company's technical research and development advancements in three trade magazines, recognizing and publicizing TelTech as a leader in the telecommunications industry.
- Assisted in developing and managing program through which community organizations received donations based on employee involvement; company contributes more than $25,000 annually to benefit its communities.

EXPERIENCE (Cont.)

| **Public Relations Administrator, Southwest Telephone, Phoenix, AZ** | **1996-1998** |

Wrote and distributed media relations materials for five-state regional telephone company.

- ▷ Served as bill insert and bill message coordinator for the entire region, including working with five state staffs to meet customer billing cycles.
- ▷ Handled media relations for company-sponsored golf tournament, including arranging press conferences, hosting and organizing the media tent, and distributing daily press releases.
- ▷ Placed three technical articles in trade magazines, enhancing company's image as a technical leader.
- ▷ Organized sponsorship of Kids Day at the Zoo, where children from low-income households visited the zoo for free; enhanced company's image in the community.

| **Senior Writer, Public Relations, Arizona Department of Commerce, Phoenix, AZ** | **1994-1996** |

Administered communications functions in the areas of agriculture, economic development, energy, and tourism. Wrote and distributed news releases about department activities.

- ▷ Wrote various agricultural and tourism speeches for Lieutenant Governor Watkins.
- ▷ Created a variety of publications, including handling photography, graphic design, and printing.
- ▷ Recommended new tourism slogan, which appeared on promotional items from T-shirts to license plates and generated $2.5M in revenue.

AWARDS/ MEMBERSHIPS

Secretary, Assistant Treasurer, Dallas Chapter, International Association of Business Communicators
- ▷ Silver Quill Award of Excellence, Special Events Program
- ▷ Silver Quill Merit Award, Special Events Program
- ▷ Silver Quill Award of Excellence, External Newsletter

Progress of Women in Communications Chair, Dallas Chapter, Women in Communications, Inc.
- ▷ Regional Competition Award of Excellence, Public Relations Campaign Series

Member, Texas Association of Event Professionals
- ▷ Honorable Mention Award, Best Promotional Item

Member, Public Relations Committee for Junior Achievement of Central Texas, Inc.

EDWARD CHANG
23 West Alamedo Blvd.
San Diego, CA 92203
(619) 555-3400
EdChang@mycomp.net

PROFILE

Manager with 10 years experience in production, supervision, and quality control. Skilled in counseling customers on quality issues, establishing quality standards, and solving quality-related problems. Capable of managing product conformance from raw material to final inspection.

EXPERIENCE

1998-present

Quality Manager, Midway Engineering, San Diego, CA
Supervise three inspectors in manufacturing of sheet metal and machine tools for major aircraft and automotive firms.
▸ Manage internal quality of manufacturing records, certifications, and requirements of individual customers.
▸ Handle internal and supplier audits and implementation of SPC.
▸ Raised quality rating with major customer from 60% to 100% in two years; no rejections in three years; resulted in Certified Supplier status and no-inspection status for goods shipped to customer from production plant.
▸ Recommended and implemented new process, which increased production by 25% without jeopardizing quality.

1995-1998

Inspection Supervisor, Tube Forming, Corp., Marshall, CA
Inspected in-process, welding, flouropenetrant, and final assembly.
▸ Handled fabrication, layout of aircraft engine tubing, and components for major aircraft companies.
▸ Implemented new inspection process, which identified and led to correction of potential defects.
▸ Helped implement mock-up thrust reverse assembly for W360 aircraft.

1993-1995

Production Supervisor, Transmission Suppliers, Inc., Marshall, CA
▸ Supervised manufacturing and grinding of friction wafers for bonding to clutch and transmission parts, meeting tolerances of ±00l.
▸ Recommended new process, resulting in fewer casting cracks, higher product quality, and $3 million in new business.
▸ Established new production procedure, which increased units produced by 35%.
▸ Wrote new quality manual, which established product specifications and standards necessary to meet customer requirements.

EDUCATION

1993

B.S. in Business Management, *With Distinction*, San Diego State University

Christina H. Chin • 809 W. Ash St. • Columbia, SC • 29230 • (803) 555-6777 • CHC@user.net

Summary of Qualifications

Nearly eight years experience in the insurance field, with emphasis on quality review. Skilled in creating, implementing, and conducting internal and external audit programs, including analyzing statistical reports, accounting reviews, and conducting staff interviews. Solid training and communication skills.

Experience

Eastern Warren, Inc., Columbia, S.C. (1997-present)
(A subsidiary of Eastern Insurance Group)

Director of Quality Review (Auditing), (1999-present)

Manage department and five professional-level employees. Audit external clients and internal staff to ensure maximum operational efficiency. Develop business plan and department budget. Handle staff training, administration and motivation.
- Create, test, and implement all audit programs.
- Continually evaluate effectiveness of audit programs and report statistics to Executive Committee.
- Identified three problem areas for major client and designed specialized audit to monitor progress, which has resulted in improved operations and work flow.

Quality Review Auditor (1997-1999)

Conducted and reported on various types of internal and external audits, encompassing a variety of operational functions in the insurance field.
- Conducted on-site aggregate claim audits to determine proper reimbursement to clients by reviewing claims, premium, eligibility, and contract interpretation.
- Conducted on-site operational audits: used statistical reports, claim, premium, accounting and eligibility reviews, and one-on-one interviews with client's staff.
- Conducted on-site approval audits, which allowed management committee to evaluate client's abilities and professional competency; used staff interviews, systems reviews, and monitored administrative techniques.

Smithton Life Insurance Company of South Carolina, Columbia, S.C.
(A subsidiary of Eastern Insurance Group)

Claims Supervisor (1995-1997)

Managed department and seven claim examiners and support staff. Administered group and individual life, disability income, and medical benefits. Developed business plan and department budget. Handled staff training and administration.
- Assisted and advised staff in making claim decisions and continually evaluated accuracy of decisions.
- Reviewed and translated insurance contracts.
- Organized and supervised daily work flows to ensure maximum productivity.
- Reduced claims response time from 30 days to two days after just six months on the job.

Education

General Studies, University of Florida, Miami (1993-1995)
- 12 credit hours in business administration

Randall R. Gibbs
935 Pheasant Run • Cheyenne, WY 82002 • (307) 555-2993 • Cell: (307) 555-2032

Skills Summary

Skilled manager with creative, innovative approach to managing staff, generating teamwork, and improving customer service. Proven track record of low turnover, low overtime, high retention rate, and high profit.

Employment

Assistant Manager/Service Manager, The Steak House, Cheyenne, WY   **2001-present**

Manage, train and schedule up to 90 employees for 250-seat restaurant, including wait staff, hostesses, bus boys and bar staff. Manage all aspects of customer service. Promoted from assistant manager to service manager in one month.

- Created monthly employee newsletter, which presents franchise policies and procedures in a nonconfrontational manner and improves knowledge of restaurant business: regional manager has recognized and adopted publication for regional use.
- Developed customer hand-out card, which explains seating procedures for large parties and provides suggested activities for guests while they wait to be seated.
- Initiated "roaming manager" approach to receive customer feedback and address problems or concerns; customer satisfaction rate currently highest in region.
- Revised and color-coded seating chart, which helps new employees learn stations and alerts kitchen staff when stations close.
- Maintain lowest overtime and turnover in region; retention rate 44% above company standard, saving $23,000 annually.
- Exceeded 2001's gross margin profits by 24%.

Kitchen Manager, The Steak House. Casper, WY   **2000-2001**

Supervised up to 20 cooks and dish area employees for 150-seat restaurant.

- Redistributed clean-up assignments to even out duties, which improved employee teamwork and morale.
- Initiated safety program, which reduced on-the-job injuries 40%; program adopted and implemented throughout region.

Head Waiter, Alpha Xi Delta Sorority, University of Wyoming, Laramie   **School year 1998-2000**

Supervised wait staff of seven and assigned serving and clean-up duties.

- Initiated recognition program, which honored wait staff for attendance and work quality; reduced high turnover/no-show rate.

Waiter/Assistant Manager, Quail Inn, Laramie, WY   **Summers 1998-2000**

Provided customer service. Filled in as assistant manager when necessary.

- Developed and implemented customer satisfaction survey, which helped improve service and increased patronage.

Education

Manager Training Program, The Steak House, Cheyenne, WY (2000)
B.S. in Restaurant/Hotel Management, University of Wyoming, Laramie (1998)

Michael Swinger
5623 North State Road 46
Advance, IA 52203
(319) 555-2034

SKILLS SUMMARY

Top salesman with extensive background in agricultural sales. Specialized technical knowledge in animal nutrition and herd management. Experienced in developing computerized record-keeping systems. Excellent analytical skills—a student of current and developing market trends. Also skilled in developing new agricultural accounts for 50,000-watt radio station. Additional experience in supervision and production management.

EMPLOYMENT

Area Sales Representative, Macon Feeds, Inc., Des Moines, IA (1999-present)
- Handle feed sales for four-county territory, generating $400,000 annually in sales.
- Recognized as one of company's top 10 salespeople each year since 1999.
- Increased number of customers by 20% in two years.
- Helped create and implement F.O.B. feed delivery system, which allowed customers to call 800 number to place an order, enhancing customer service and increasing territory sales by 25%.
- Implemented computerized swine record-keeping program, resulting in better report generation and improved feed analysis and herd management.

Agricultural Account Representative, AAAA Radio, Linden, IA (1995-1999)
- Handled 40 agricultural accounts in the 40-mile radius listening area (50,000 watts).
- Developed 10 new accounts in last year with the station.
- Improved national account status by 30%.
- Managed $250,000 sales budget
- Organized weekend radio auctions and supervised staff of three who obtained price-reduced or donated items/services from local businesses, resulting in profitable air time for the station and positive advertising results for the businesses.

Sales Representative, Holmstead Mills, Inc., Davenport, IA (1991-1995)
- Handled feed sales for two counties, generating $250,000 in annual sales.
- Counseled customers on feed products and nutrition management.
- Assisted customers in assessing feed needs and developing goals.
- Achieved top salesperson status (first in 1995), earning four incentive trips.
- Served on team to develop company's computerized record-keeping system, resulting in more accurate customer records and improved product sales and account analysis.

Shift Supervisor, Third Shift Superintendent, American Chain Co., Des Moines, IA (1989-1991)
- Supervised up to 200 union employees in manufacturing facility.
- Managed production, disciplinary action, budget, material handling, safety, and quality control.
- Promoted after one year to superintendent.
- Implemented and assisted industrial engineering department in layout and moving of heavy chain assembly to another area of the plant, resulting in a smooth transition and only four hours of production down time (budgeted time was 12 hours).
- Revised and implemented new procedure in assembly department, resulting in productivity increase of 25%.

Supervisor, National Filters, Warren, IA (1986-1989)
- Supervised up to 30 union employees in a production plant.
- Worked with human resources department to design a new safety program, reducing on-the-job injuries by 30%.
- Recommended new product and distribution system, which opened up business opportunities in three new market areas.

EDUCATION

Graduate Studies in Economics and Marketing, Iowa State University (1999-2000)
Bachelor of Science Degree in Business Management, University of Iowa (1986)

RELATED AFFILIATIONS

Director, White County Pork Producers, White County, IA (1999-current)
Officer, Consignment Sale Chairman, White County Young Farmers, White County, IA (2000-current)
- Established and organize annual consignment sale with high school vocational agricultural department.
- Raise nearly $3,000 annually.

THERESA KNAPP

401 Hunter's Way
Hewes, CA 92182

(619) 555-2003
TerryK@hayoo.com

SKILLS SUMMARY   Award-winning account executive with strong background in computer system sales, multi-national territory management, end-user prospecting, competitive engagements, complex contract negotiations, and third-party software partnerships. Excellent experience in financial analysis and in forecasting sales revenue, volume, discounting, and profit. Proven ability to consistently exceed sales goals.

PC application skills: Windows, Word, Excel, PowerPoint

WORK EXPERIENCE

Major Account Executive, Advanced Computer Systems, Reading, CA   **2001-present**
Develop new territory in district, including several Fortune 500 accounts, such as
Levi Strauss and Esprit.

- Market and sell large-scale UNIX and Windows NT symmetric multiprocessing servers and professional services as solutions for companies moving from proprietary to open systems.
- Generate prospects for applications, including manufacturing, financials, decision support, enterprise messaging, and enterprise architecture planning.
- Prospect for new business through various marketing campaigns, including telemarketing, direct mail, targeted seminars and partnerships with leading software firms.
- Recommended new territory-management approach, which netted 15 new clients and a 45% sales increase.

Marketing & Finance Staff, PFE Corp., Los Angeles, CA   **1999-2001**
Promoted to staff assignment to broaden experience and prepare for sales management.

- Handled financial analysis and planning for $4 billion Western U.S. sales and services.
- Forecasted sales revenue, volumes, discounting, and profit for company vice president.
- Assigned sales quota to 20 regional managers, covering 10 states.
- Earned two Finance Director's awards for forecasting and sales quota management.

WORK EXPERIENCE

International Account Manager, PFE Corp., Los Angeles, CA　　　　　**1995-1999**

Managed worldwide $10 million sales quota for Fortune 500 account, including complete line of products and services. Handled sales volume of more than $25 million.

- Directed $500,000 3-D apparel CAD application to reduce time-to-market delays and enhance retail sales operations.
- Ranked in top three of PFE's 30 sales representatives.
- Posted 110% to 135% quota performance with four consecutive 100% Clubs.
- Earned Regional Manager's award for first new $5 million mainframe at Fortune 500 company.
- Won competitive bids over other major computer product and service providers, including AT&T and IBM.

Manufacturing Management, PFE Corp., Los Angeles, CA　　　　　**1990-1995**

Supervised technical activities and 30 employees at company production plant.

- Designed manufacturing facilities, planned capital budgets, and presented investment business cases to plant manager.
- Consistently exceeded production schedules while achieving 99.5% defect-free quality.
- Evaluated and recommended new process which helped plant exceed production objectives while 15% understaffed.
- Earned Outstanding Manager's award for leading department's turnaround success.

EDUCATION　　　　B.S., Industrial Engineering, *Cum Laude,* California Polytechnical Institute

ACTIVITIES　　　　Fundraising Chairman, Kappa Kappa Kappa philanthrophic organization
Advisor, Junior Achievement Club of Hewes, CA

TAMMY OBERFORCE

45 Tacoma Dr.
East Bend, NM 87033

(505) 555-2003
www.toberforce.net/homepage

SKILLS PROFILE

- Ten years experience in retail sales, including purchasing, inventory management, and advertising.
- Skilled in developing successful sales promotions.
- Experienced in training and managing sales staffs.
- Skilled in customer account management.
- Strong computer skills.

EMPLOYMENT HISTORY

Department Manager, McKesson Hardware and Gifts, Mesa, AZ (1999-present)
- Manage purchasing and inventory for housewares department, which generates annual sales of $250,000.
- Introduced and handled sales promotions for new housewares product line, resulting in increased sales of 30%.
- Initiated new advertising strategies, which enhanced customer image of store and increased customer traffic.
- Worked with other local retailers to establish "Summer Sizzle Sidewalk Day," including retailer discounts, craft booths, and fund-raising activities for local civic organizations.
- Design and arrange window display for housewares section.
- Manage staff of three and train all new sales employees.

Sales Clerk/Bookkeeper, McKesson Hardware and Gifts, Mesa, AZ (1996-1999)
- Handled floor sales for housewares and gift departments.
- Organized special holiday sales promotion and recommended special holiday gift line, which increased sales by 35%.
- Established new accounts, posted accounts receivable and prepared and sent monthly statements.
- Reviewed past-due accounts with clients and established payment plans.
- Recommended computerized bookkeeping and supervised all data entry, resulting in reduced bookkeeping time, detailed department reports, improved sales projections, and enhanced business, advertising, and budget planning.

Sales Clerk, Sears, Roebuck & Co., Mesa, AZ (Summers 1992-1996)
- Handled floor and cash register sales in hardware, paint, and housewares departments.
- Assisted in training new sales clerks.
- Suggested new display idea for housewares product, which improved customers' view of—and accessibility to—the product, resulting in increased sales.

EDUCATION

Graduate, Mesa Community High School, Mesa, AZ (1996)

Kevin C. Myers
1112 Somerset Ct. Burlington, VT • 05406 • (802) 555-6223 • KevinCM@mailstar.net

Skills Profile

More than 20 years of teaching and administrative experience. Skilled in encouraging and supporting restructuring efforts and moving the decision-making process closer to the classroom. Solid background in developing a variety of learning environments that actively engage students.

Work Experience
1996-present

Superintendent of Schools, Burlington Community School Corporation, Burlington, VT
- Initiated and implemented several school reform projects, including year-round school education (2001), and the only integrated, thematic elementary school in the eastern third of the country (2000).
- Earned Smithton Award for Innovation in Education (2001).
- Spearheaded several district-wide technology projects, including integrating computer technology and video information systems and implementing long-distance interactive learning programs at high-school level.
- Initiated and implemented two building renovation programs, averaging $25M each.
- Worked with staff and school board members in multi-faceted, professional development program based on effective school research.

1990-1996

Assistant Superintendent of Schools, Montpelier Community School Corporation, Montpelier, VT
- Managed business operations and fiscal services.
- Handled teacher collective bargaining, district budget preparation and contract management.
- Developed alternative learning programs for at-risk students in grades K-12, which successfully oriented them to the learning process.
- Promoted and facilitated funded grant proposals, with revenue exceeding $1M in six years, resulting in innovative curricular programs.

1988-1990

Director of Instruction and Curriculum, Montpelier Community School Corporation, Montpelier, VT
- Supervised curriculum development and management of K-12 instructional programs.
- Revised and modified achievement testing and formative evaluation of all instructional programs for the corporation, which better reflected students' progress in innovative curriculum.

Work Experience

1986-1988   **Building Level Administrator**, Brackett Middle School, Richmond Community School System, Richmond, VA
- Managed all activities in 1,200-student, open-spaced middle school (grades 6-8).
- Implemented differential staffing model, using instructional assistants and teacher interns.

1981-1986   **Classroom Teacher**, Richmond Community School System, Richmond, VA
- Instructed eighth- and ninth-grade classes in chemistry and biology.
- Developed instructional television project, involving programming for biological sciences

Education

Doctorate of Education, University of Vermont, Montpelier (1990)
Educational Specialist Degree, University of Virginia, Richmond (1987)
Master of Arts in Education, University of Virginia, Richmond (1983)
Bachelor of Arts in Biology, University of Virginia, Richmond (1981)

Licensing

Vermont—Superintendent (Professional)
Virginia—State Teacher, Superintendent

Professional Activities

Member, American Association of School Administrators
Member, Association of Supervision and Curriculum Development
Member, Vermont Association of Public School Superintendents
Member, Vermont Association of School Business Officials
Member, State Education Task Force
- Designed new Principal Preparation Model
- Developed state's Center for Creativity

Community Activities

Treasurer, Tri-County Mental Health Association
Member, Rotary Club

KENNETH G. LAMBERT

2015 Park St. • Boseman, MT • 59715 • (406) 555-0224 • www.Kenneth_Lambert_home.com

OBJECTIVE To secure capital and investors for business expansion.

PROFILE Award-winning business owner with more than seven years experience in management, marketing, sales, and training. Skilled in determining, developing, and securing funding for successful business growth.

EXPERIENCE

1997-present **Owner, Gadgets, Gifts & Gear, Bozeman, MT**
Own and manage business, which provides variety of hardware, gifts, and clothing. Handle all aspects of business, including customer service, sales, purchasing, accounting, and employee hiring and training.
- Expanded hardware line in 1999 to include small appliances and gifts, which nearly doubled sales in one year.
- Grew business from two employees and annual sales of $300K to 12 employees and annual sales of $1.5M in three years.
- Tapped into tourist trade in 2001 by offering quality, name-brand outdoor clothing and fishing supplies, which increased sales 20%.

1995-1997 **Manager, Clem's Camping Supplies, Bozeman, MT**
Supervised all floor sales and trained sales staff. Managed inventory, purchasing, and customer service.
- Assisted owner in enhancing store's physical appearance, which increased customer traffic.
- Introduced new line of protective gear, which increased sales 35% in one year.

1993-1995 **River Guide, Fly Fishing Tours, Inc., Bozeman, MT**
Led group fly fishing tours, including five-day, overnight camping trips.
- Earned Top Guide Award 1994-1995.

PROFESSIONAL ORGANIZATIONS
Vice President, Northwest America Hardware Association
- Help determine services for all hardware stores in five-state area.
- Named Outstanding Store Manager—Growth (2000).

Board Member, Young Hardware Professionals
- Currently working on networking program to assist young hardware professionals.

ACTIVITIES Parade Committee Chairman, Bozeman Fall Festival

EDUCATION Business courses, University of Montana, Helena (1991-1993)

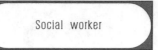
Social worker

Nancy Stetson • 45 Valley Ridge Rd. • Willow, NE • 68023 • (402) 555-9203 • NStetson@alo.net

SUMMARY OF QUALIFICATIONS

Nearly 10 years experience in social work, including administration, supervision, and training. Excellent background in assisting emotionally/behaviorally disturbed children and their families. Experienced in developing and implementing treatment plans and services and working with the community, local referral agencies, and school systems. Skilled in fund raising and event planning. Accustomed to successfully juggling several responsibilities simultaneously.

WORK EXPERIENCE

Admissions Social Worker, Nebraska Lutheran Children's Home, Willow, NE   2000 - present

Receive and coordinate referrals for admissions to the agency. Schedule and conduct pre-admission and diagnostic assessments. Serve as liaison with referral sources such as the County Division of Family and Children/Welfare, courts, parents, and schools.

- Schedule and conduct in-service training for various staff, including child care workers, social workers, and on-grounds school teachers.
- Serve as co-leader for treatment groups, including anger management, survivors of molestation, and children of alcoholics.
- Worked with local church music department to create choir from children's home; choir performs monthly during worship service; membership has grown from 15 to 42; social workers have documented increased self-esteem and improved group interaction skills among choir members.
- Assisted public relations manager in revising annual fund-raiser used with Lutheran churches across the country, which resulted in a 20% increase in donations.

Social Worker, Nebraska Lutheran Children's Home, Willow, NE   1996 - 2000

Developed and implemented treatment plans and services for emotionally/behaviorally disturbed girls and their families. Provided written and verbal progress reports to placing agencies, including testifying at court hearings. Provided individual, group, and family counseling.

- Worked with families to determine appropriate communication and limit-setting in the home.
- Met with public school personnel to assess residents' ongoing educational needs.
- Organized and chaired for three years an auction of goods donated from local businesses and community residents, which raised more than $10,000 annually.

Child Care Worker, Smithton Home for Girls, Rockville, NE   1993 - 1996

Supervised daily activities of residents, including housekeeping, leisure, and recreational time and study time. Observed residents' behavior, noting changes, significant incidents, both positive and negative.

- Established and maintained a working relationship with each resident's social worker.
- Created fund-raising event that brought in more than $2,500 annually.

EDUCATION/CERTIFICATION

Bachelor of Arts, University of Nebraska, Lincoln (1993)
Majors: Psychology and Sociology

Certified Social Worker, State of Nebraska (1993)

MONICA HARRISON
101 Sonnet Lane
Eagleton, WA 99002
(509) 555-7209
MonicaHa@mail.net

SUMMARY OF QUALIFICATIONS

- More than 10 years of tax and accounting research and experience.
- Thorough knowledge of all types of taxes and tax and financial issues.
- Experienced in establishing corporate tax department and 401k plan.
- Skilled in preparing corporate and personal tax returns, with specialized background in pension plans, not-for-profit organizations, farms and consolidated, multi-state corporate returns.
- Strong administrative experience.

PROFESSIONAL EXPERIENCE

1999-present   **Tax Manager, American North Airlines, Seattle, WA**
Administer all functions relating to federal, state, and local income, excise, property, and transaction taxes, as well as foreign value-added taxes. Review and assist in preparing all tax accruals and tax account balance sheet reconciliations. Review all payroll tax returns.

- Identify and analyze the tax effects of all company transactions, including the establishment and purchase of subsidiaries, ensuring positive business decisions.
- Recommend necessary changes in internal procedures to comply with tax law changes.
- Provide guidance to the Human Resources Department with respect to fringe benefits, including 401k plan.
- Helped develop and implement "cafeteria-style" benefits plan, which provides employees with a variety of benefits and enhances the company's benefits package.

1997-1999   **Tax Staff Accountant, American North Airlines, Seattle, WA**
- Developed a tax department for the company, including completing research and developing all tax functions, resulting in substantial annual savings previously paid to an outside tax consulting firm.
- Established a 401k plan for company employees, enhancing the company's benefit package.
- Performed non-tax-related duties, such as compiling projections and helping analyze financial decisions.

PROFESSIONAL EXPERIENCE

1994-1997

Tax Senior, Whitlatch and Henry, Seattle, WA
- Prepared and reviewed individual, partnership, and corporate returns, including consolidated and multi-state corporate returns.
- Specialized in research, compilation of financial projections, business valuations, and interstate taxation (income and transaction taxes).
- Trained other staff tax preparers on new computer software, saving $4,500 in outside training costs.

1993-1994

Tax Senior, Turner McDonald & Co., San Diego, CA
- Supervised and trained newer staff members.
- Specialized in pension plans, not-for-profit organizations, farms, and consolidated, multi-state corporate returns.
- Recommended new computer software which reduced manual computation time and increased productivity.

1992-1993

Staff Accountant, Turner McDonald & Co., San Diego, CA
- Prepared various tax returns and researched tax issues.
- Revised intern program, resulting in increased productivity for company and broader experience for interns.

1991-1991

Audit Intern, Turner McDonald & Co., San Diego, CA
- Assisted with four audits and performed a complete audit of a political action committee.

EDUCATION

1991

University of Northern California, San Diego
Bachelor of Science in Accounting

PROFESSIONAL AFFILIATIONS

1997-present	Tax Executives Institute
2001-2002	▹ Chapter Director
2000-2001	▹ Membership Committee Chairperson
2000-present	Northwest CPA Society
2002	▹ Regional Representative
2001-present	National Tax Accountants Network

RELATED VOLUNTEER WORK

2000-present	Senior Services Center, Eagleton, WA
	▹ Provide tax preparation and tax consulting for senior citizens
1998-2000	First Christian Church
	▹ Treasurer

Abigail Scott

45 Stone Court
Williamsburg, PA 17704

(717) 555-4554
A_Scott@elementary.edu

CAREER OBJECTIVE

To secure a full-time teaching position at the kindergarten to 3rd-grade level.

SKILLS PROFILE

▸ Develop and implement lesson plans for all areas of a developmentally appropriate curriculum.
▸ Create and initiate hands-on learning experiences.
▸ Design and implement integrated learning centers.
▸ Advise and counsel parents on their child's specific cognitive or emotional problems.
▸ Coordinate with other teachers on special school programs.

EMPLOYMENT HISTORY

Third Grade Teacher, Briggs Elementary School, Frankfort, PA   **1996 - present**
▸ Created and implemented "Guest Reader" program, where local officials and business people visit the classroom to read books to the students, building a positive relationship between the school and community and introducing students to civic leaders.
▸ Developed learning center on dinosaurs for 1st- through 3rd-grade students, which earned State Teacher's Association recognition for combining math, history, and science in a primary school project.
▸ Helped coordinate and implement home/school electronic mail network, which allows parents and teachers to communicate via computer to verify homework assignments, follow up on previous communication, and discuss a student's progress; network has resulted in increased parent communication and classroom participation and improved school work among students.
▸ Coordinate annual school Christmas program and all 3rd-grade field trips.

Kindergarten Teacher, Warren Elementary School, Williamsburg, PA   **1994 - 1996**
▸ Secured grant for classroom computer and created computer learning center, which introduced students to computers and prepared them for future school assignments.
▸ Initiated special classroom projects, resulting in increased parent participation in the classroom.
▸ Created "Animals in our World" program, which introduced students to rare and endangered animals and their habitats.

Substitute Teacher, Warren County School Corporation, Williamsburg, PA   **1993 - 1994**
▸ Guided students (elementary through high school) through lessons set by teacher.
▸ Served on team that created substitute teacher manual, resulting in standardized procedures for common classroom situations and problems.

EMPLOYMENT HISTORY

Student Teacher, Washington Elementary School, Washington, PA   1993 - 1993
- Worked two months with kindergarten students and two months in a 3rd-grade classroom.
- Modified lessons for and streamlined two learning disabled children into regular curriculum.
- Created reading center for 3rd-grade classroom, which provided activities and reading materials for students who finished their school work before others.
- Assisted in after-school tutor program.

Teaching Assistant, Lil Tikes Nursery School, Washington, PA   1990 - 1993
- Stimulated the creativity in children through various art and creative dance projects.
- Guided children through problems by positive verbal and nonverbal interactions.
- Initiated role playing as a way to learn to solve problems.

Swimming Instructor, YMCA, Washington, PA   1986 - present
- Instruct children ages 2 to 14 in beginning and intermediate swimming and water safety skills.
- Work with 150 children each summer.

EDUCATION

Bachelor of Science Degree, Early Childhood Education, Pennsylvania State University, *with honors* (1989)

EDUCATIONAL ACTIVITIES

Cheevers County Community School System
- Parents' Council, Community Action Committee
- Secretary, Elementary School Improvement Team

State Computers in the Classroom Association (past president, current committee chair)

OTHER INSTRUCTIONAL ACTIVITIES

Sunday School teacher, St. Thomas Church, Williamsburg, PA
Leader for Child Care 4-H Project, Cheevers County, PA
Little League Coach, Williamsburg, PA

LOUISE T. SHEPHERD
910 Crescent Dr.
Marion, NV 89113
(702) 555-0173
LTShepherd@school.edu

SKILLS PROFILE

- Five years experience teaching special education students.
- Certified in instructing the emotionally handicapped, learning disabled, and mildly mentally handicapped.
- Experienced in placing eligible special education students in regular classrooms.
- Skilled in developing and improving students' social skills and successfully addressing behavioral problems.
- Adept in conducting case conferences and working with parents.

EMPLOYMENT HISTORY

Williams County School District, Marion, NV

Special Services Teacher, Lincoln High School (2000-present)
Instruct up to 10 emotionally handicapped (EH), learning disabled (LD), and mildly mentally handicapped (MIMH) students. Work with MIMH and EH students in self-contained classroom and place eligible LD students in regular classrooms through inclusionary program.

- Develop individualized lesson plans for each student in self-contained classroom.
- Implemented inclusionary program and guide general education teachers in modifying curriculum to address special education students' abilities.
- Assisted four MIMH students in earning passing grades in regular biology.
- Developed and implemented Individual Evaluation Program, which requires teacher of record to write individual evaluations on each student and share results with parents.

Teaching Assistant, Lincoln High School (1998-2000)
Assisted special services staff with students at various learning levels (MIMH, EH, LD). Assisted general education teachers in modifying lessons. Created curriculum for special education students grades 9–11. Counseled students on behavioral and social problems.

- Instructed inclusionary classes in English and physical science.
- Worked one-on-one with three MIMH students, evaluated their progress and conducted parent conferences.

WORK EXPERIENCE

Williams County School District, Marion, NV

> **Homebound Tutor (1998-2000)**
> Created curriculum in all areas for two middle school and two high school students (MIMH, EH). Counseled students on behavioral and emotional issues.

Pine City Community School Corporation, Pine City, NV

> **Student Teacher, Pine City High School (1998)**
> Worked eight weeks with general education students and eight weeks with special education students in grades 9–12. Designed various lesson plans and coordinated several unit plans. Assisted general education teachers in modifying lesson plans for special education students.
>
> : Worked one-on-one with three LD and EH students in self-contained classroom and guided and assisted one LD student in regular classrooms.

EDUCATION/CERTIFICATION

Bachelor of Science, University of Nevada, Carson City (1998)
> Major; Special Education
> Minor: Secondary Education

Certified Instructor, LD/EH/MIMH, University of Nevada, Carson City (1999)

EDUCATIONAL MEMBERSHIPS

Member, Nevada Association of Special Education Teachers
Member, Fundraising Committee, Williams County Education Foundation

ACTIVITIES

Volunteer, Marion Public Library, Marion, NY

MARISSA HANDLON
35 West Parker Way
Henderson, NJ 07553
www.Handlon22.com

(201) 555-5039

Fax: (201) 555-9712

SKILLS SUMMARY
Software and hardware expert with more than 10 years of experience in project planning and management, program management, and systems integration. Strong background in telecommunications applications. Experienced in integrating internal computer services and needs into the business planning process. Skilled in training and team building, including identifying problems and designing solutions. Adept at working with interdependent departments and organizations to develop and implement program plans.

EDUCATION
MBA, Marketing/Finance, Northwestern University (1999)
BS, Computer Science, Michigan State University (1993)

WORK EXPERIENCE

Technical Director, Public Communications, Atlantic Tel, Rochester, NJ   **2000-current**
Manage operations of software development and maintenance team.

- Developed and started three-year plan to consolidate and upgrade obsolete UNIX minicomputer hardware and convert mission critical production software to the new platform.
- Managed the hardware and network procurement and installation across several business units, assessing and redesigning existing production systems to better fit changing business needs.
- Restructured software development team to increase productivity and build individual technical skills.
- Implemented a quarterly performance feedback process and reinforced basic project management processes.
- Addressed chronic maintenance problems and increasing internal user demand for services by actively working with senior management to highlight technical issues.
- Results of analysis included funding for a disaster planning project, implementation of a PC-based application for finance group to demonstrate end-user computing, and creation of a systems support team as a member of the annual business planning process.

WORK EXPERIENCE

Senior Manager, Davis Consulting, Chicago, IL   **1993-2000**
Managed small- to large-systems projects, from proposal to full implementation.

Project Planning and Management
Regional Telephone Company
➤ Developed multi-year project phasing strategy across several interdependent organizations to achieve benefits as early as possible by identifying palatable phasing strategies, negotiating with individual projects to determine feasibility, identifying dependences, and developing action plan.
➤ Supervised the development of the conversion plan, including preparing the technical design, estimating the detail design and manual conversion efforts, developing the master conversion schedule to match a phased implementation, and obtaining approval from affected departments.
➤ Managed the development of field support software for sales representatives and developed opportunity to jointly market the software to other local exchange carriers.

Project Management
Large Personal Computer Manufacturer
➤ Achieved management consensus on action plan for funds and commissions project by defining feasible alternatives, negotiating approach across several internal organizations, and gaining approval for implementation tasks.
➤ Completed requirements phase, including documenting key features and functions, reviewing and obtaining approval of documentation, and defining an implementation approach.

Systems Integration
County Human Services Agency
➤ Managed the technical architecture team that designed and developed the county's expert system/workstation-based welfare eligibility system and determined the feasibility of the multi-vendor hardware/software solution.
➤ Successfully developed and managed complex implementation schedule which incorporated procuring $3.5M in hardware and software, selecting a site preparation vendor, installing a 350-workstation network across three sites, coordinating mainframe installation, and training 350 users.

ACTIVITIES   Secretary, Michigan State University Alumnae, New Jersey Chapter
Volunteer/Computer Operations Advisor, Henderson Boys' and Girls' Club

ROSA B. ORTIZ
422 W. Ridge Rd.
Kansas City, KS 66136
(913) 555-0090
Rosaortiz@access.net

SKILLS SUMMARY

Manager and corporate trainer with solid background in developing training programs and computer software materials. Skilled in providing hands-on field service and ensuring client satisfaction. Extensive insurance and marketing experience.

WORK HISTORY
2001-current

Training and Field Service Manager
AllNet Financial Corp.
Kansas City, KS

Train medical and dental providers on patient finance program and practice management software. Serve as liaison between providers, sales staff and administrative staff.

➤ Developed all corporate training and marketing materials for medical financing program and practice management software.
➤ Designed and assisted with software programming, which supports current products.
➤ Evaluate client needs and conform policies and procedures to best suit client needs, while staying within legal and operational constraints.
➤ Communicate with clients to ensure satisfaction with program and provide education to resolve potential conflicts.

1998-2001

Corporate Trainer
West Bend Mutual Insurance Company
Lawrence, KS

Provided training for headquarters executives and professionals in 50 branch offices throughout the country.

➤ Developed and maintained a series of training manuals and tests, which were used to evaluate the continued employment of the student.
➤ Conducted several classroom-style training sessions for specific technical functions.
➤ Created self-study program, which increased productivity by allowing student to study outside of classroom.

WORK HISTORY

1996-1998

Client Service Supervisor
West Bend Mutual Insurance Company
Lawrence, KS

Supervised department of 18 service representatives that received all incoming client inquiries.
➤ Reduced client response time from 60 days to one day in just two months.
➤ Established first-ever comprehensive training program, which resulted in a more productive and efficient staff.

1995-1996

Marketing Promotions Manager
Walters Marketing, Inc.
Kansas City, MO

Generated sales leads for major recreational manufacturer. Located and negotiated exhibit areas in trade shows, malls, and fairs in tri-state area.
➤ Selected to travel to other branch locations to hire, train, and motivate new managers.
➤ Consistently increased leads by 46% through effective management techniques.
➤ Earned Manager of the Year award (1995).

EDUCATION

University of Kansas, Lawrence
➤ 18 hours of graduate studies in management and training (1998-2000)
➤ Bachelor of Science in Marketing (1994)

ACTIVITIES

Publicity Committee, Kansas City Arts Alliance
Big Sister, Tri-County Big Sisters, Inc.

Writer

LISA J. BLEVINS

901 W. State Road 41   (402) 555-2331
Willow, NE. 68505   Blevins@mailser.net

SUMMARY OF SKILLS

- Ten years of experience in professional news writing, feature writing, and copy editing.
- Ability to write accurately and effectively about a wide range of subject matter.
- Skilled in interviewing, research, and photography.
- Adept in determining the "hook" that creates the strongest connection between the story and the audience.

WORK HISTORY

1997-present   **Writer/Editor, Independent School Management, Willow, Neb.**
- Edit all custom publications, including viewbooks and direct mail brochures, that reflect unique, individual programs of each school.
- Co-lead "Marketing Your School" and lead "Powerful Public Relations" workshops, which assist schools in presenting a specific image through admission materials, newsletters, advertising, and working with the media.
- Create in-house marketing materials, such as catalogs, brochures, and flyers, which have led to increased attendance at company workshops.
- Established and edit company's signature publication, which has repeatedly earned national recognition among independent school administrators and educators.

2000-present   **Owner, Blevins Communications, Willow, Neb.**
- Created and edit Willow School District monthly newsletter and annual report, and handle all research, writing, graphics, design, typesetting, and printing arrangements.
- Create brochures and flyers for local businesses and nonprofit organizations.

1992-1997   **Reporter/Managing Editor, The Frankfort Times, Frankfort, Neb.**
- Covered every type of story, from club activities and police reports to feature articles and major community news.
- Promoted to managing editor March 1995.
- Wrote editorials, columns, and reviews, and edited correspondents' copy.
- Earned eight Nebraska journalism awards for writing.

EDUCATION
1992   Bachelor of Arts Degree in Journalism, University of Nebraska, Lincoln

ACTIVITIES
1999-present   Volunteer, Lincoln Arts Alliance